MACMILLAN READERS
INTERMEDIATE LEVEL

JANE AUSTEN

Pride and Prejudice

Retold by Margaret Tarner

MACMILLAN

MACMILLAN READERS
INTERMEDIATE LEVEL

Founding Editor: John Milne

The Macmillan Readers provide a choice of enjoyable reading materials for learners of English. The series is published at six levels – Starter, Beginner, Elementary, Pre-intermediate, Intermediate and Upper.

Level control
Information, structure and vocabulary are controlled to suit the students' ability at each level.

The number of words at each level:

Starter	about 300 basic words
Beginner	about 600 basic words
Elementary	about 1100 basic words
Pre-intermediate	about 1400 basic words
Intermediate	about 1600 basic words
Upper	about 2200 basic words

Vocabulary
Some difficult words and phrases in this book are important for understanding the story. Some of these words are explained in the story and some are shown in the pictures. From Pre-intermediate level upwards, words are marked with a number like this: …[3]. These words are explained in the Glossary at the end of the book.

Contents

	A Note About the Author	4
1	New Neighbours	5
2	Mrs Bennet's Plan	11
3	The Bennets Have a Visitor	19
4	The Netherfield Ball	25
5	Mr Collins Finds a Wife	30
6	Jane Loses All Hope	36
7	Elizabeth Visits Hunsford	41
8	Mr Darcy Speaks	47
9	The Militia Goes to Brighton	53
10	Elizabeth in Derbyshire	58
11	Bad News	65
12	Mr and Mrs George Wickham	69
13	Mr Bingley Returns to Netherfield	74
14	Lady Catherine Asks Some Questions	77
15	'My Dear, Dear Lizzy!'	81
	Points for Understanding	88
	Glossary	91

A Note About the Author

Jane Austen was born in 1775 at Steventon, Hampshire, in the south of England. Jane's father worked in the church in Steventon. He made sure that his children had a good education.

In 1803 Jane and her family moved to Bath in the west of England. Jane was not happy. Some people think that she had an unhappy love affair there.

In 1807 the family moved to Southampton on the south coast. In 1810 the family moved again, to Chawton, in Hampshire. From that year until her death in 1817 Jane was very busy. She wrote books, she visited her relatives and she travelled round England with friends. Jane Austen never got married. From her diaries and letters we can see that she was a very kind and intelligent woman.

In 1811 her first book was published. Her books were published without her name on them. Not many women writers were published at this time. Publishers preferred to publish books by men.

Her books are: *Sense and Sensibility* (1811), *Pride and Prejudice* (1813), *Mansfield Park* (1814), *Emma* (1815), *Northanger Abbey* (1818), *Persuasion* (1818), *Sanditon* (unfinished).

Jane Austen wrote about people who had money and property (houses and land). Some people were richer than others, but none of them were poor. These people did not work. They visited each other and they met at balls and dances. They played cards and read books and had conversations.

Men got money and property from their fathers. An eldest son usually got most of the money and property after his father's death. Younger sons often went into the church or the army. Daughters stayed at home. They learnt to read and write, to draw, play music and sew. It was important for a girl to marry a man who had money and property.

In this society, people were very polite and formal. They used Mr, Miss or Mrs unless they knew each other very well, eg 'Miss Jane', 'Mr Darcy'. People travelled in carriages pulled by horses or walked, but women did not usually go out alone.

1
New Neighbours

Everyone knows that a rich, unmarried man needs a pretty wife. And every mother wants her daughters to be happily married.

Mr and Mrs Bennet of Longbourn House, in the village of Longbourn, had five unmarried daughters. So when Mrs Bennet heard that a young man was coming to live in the neighbourhood[1], she was delighted[2]. She found out all she could about him, and hurried to tell her husband the good news.

'Oh, Mr Bennet, Netherfield Hall is let[3] at last!' Mrs Bennet cried excitedly. 'Don't you want to know who is going to live there?'

'No,' Mr Bennet answered, 'but I am sure you want to tell me.'

'The house is let to a young man from the north of England. His name is Bingley, he's very rich and not married. What a chance this is[4] for our dear Jane! Everyone knows she's the most beautiful girl in Hertfordshire. She's so good-natured[5] too. She will be an excellent wife for Mr Bingley.

'I shall be very happy to have her living so near us. And in a fine[6] house like Netherfield too! Mr Bingley plans to live there with his sister. She and Jane —'

'Please stop a moment, Mrs Bennet,' her husband said quietly. 'Why are you telling me all this? Mr Bingley is a stranger. But you are saying that he has come here to marry one of our daughters!'

'I did not say that,' Mrs Bennet answered. 'But we must think of our daughters' future. You must call on[7] Mr Bingley at once, Mr Bennet.'

'I don't think so, my dear,' Mr Bennet said calmly[8]. 'But I'll write to this young man and give him my permission to marry Jane – or whoever he chooses. Perhaps he'd like to marry my little Lizzy.'

'Don't tease[9] me, please, Mr Bennet,' Mrs Bennet replied. 'I

New Neighbours

know Lizzy is your favourite daughter, but she is not as beautiful as Jane, nor as lively as Lydia.'

'Our girls are silly and thoughtless,' Mr Bennet said severely[10]. 'But Lizzy is a little more sensible[11] than the others.'

Mr and Mrs Bennet were not happily married. After twenty-three years, Mr Bennet was tired of his wife's chatter and love of gossip[12]. And Mrs Bennet had never understood her husband's sense of humour[13].

A few days later, Mr Bennet called on Mr Bingley, without telling Mrs Bennet. She was delighted when she found out that Mr Bennet had called at Netherfield Hall.

'Girls, you have such a good father!' Mrs Bennet cried. 'You will thank him for calling at Netherfield, Jane, when you are married to Mr Bingley.

'You must look very beautiful at the next assembly ball[14], my dear,' Mrs Bennet went on, 'I'm sure that Mr Bingley will be there.'

On the following Friday, the assembly rooms in the town of Meryton were crowded. Everyone stared as Mr Bingley came in with two ladies and two gentlemen.

The fashionably dressed young woman with Mr Bingley was his unmarried sister, Miss Caroline Bingley. Mr Bingley's married sister, Louisa Hurst, was also there, with her husband. The other gentleman was Mr Bingley's friend, Mr Fitzwilliam Darcy.

Mr Bingley was a good-looking young man with a pleasant smile. Mr Darcy was tall, very handsome and from a noble family[15]. People said he had twice as much money as Mr Bingley and a large estate[16] in Derbyshire. He was also unmarried.

At first, everyone admired[17] Mr Darcy. But he danced only with Bingley's sisters and spoke to no one else. Mrs Bennet and her friends soon agreed that, although Mr Darcy was a fine gentleman, he was much too proud[18].

However, Mr Bingley pleased everyone. And Mrs Bennet was delighted when he danced with Jane.

Elizabeth Bennet watched Jane and Mr Bingley. Her dark eyes were shining with pleasure.

New Neighbours

'Darcy, why aren't you dancing?' Bingley called to his friend. 'There are plenty of pretty girls here tonight.'

'You are dancing with the only beautiful woman in the room,' Mr Darcy replied.

'But one of Miss Jane Bennet's pretty sisters is without a dancing partner,' Bingley answered. 'I will ask Jane to introduce you to her.'

Darcy looked at Elizabeth, who was standing near him. They looked at each other for a moment and then Darcy turned away.

'She is quite pretty, but not beautiful enough to interest me,' Darcy said coldly.

Elizabeth was amused[19]. She repeated the conversation to all her friends. When Mrs Bennet heard what Darcy had said she was very angry.

'That man thinks he is too good for us!' Mrs Bennet cried. 'Don't worry, Lizzy. One day, Mr Darcy will ask you to dance. When he does, refuse to dance with him!'

Elizabeth laughed.

'I shall never dance with Mr Darcy,' she said. 'He is a very proud man. I have decided to dislike him.'

Kitty and Lydia, the youngest of the Bennet girls, had a much happier time than Elizabeth. A militia regiment[20] was staying in Meryton for the winter. The officers were at the ball wearing their smart red coats. Kitty and Lydia danced with the young soldiers all evening.

Jane Bennet, too, had a very happy time.

'I admire Mr Bingley,' Jane told Elizabeth quietly when they were at home again. 'He has such fine manners[21]. And we agreed about everything.'

'You are so good-natured that you think everyone else is good-natured too,' Elizabeth answered. 'But I think Mr Bingley is a very pleasant young man. You have my permission to fall in love with him!'

Jane blushed[22] and smiled.

'Mr Bingley is very different from Mr Darcy. I am surprised they

'She is quite pretty, but not beautiful enough to interest me,' Darcy said coldly.

New Neighbours

are friends,' she said. 'Poor Lizzy. He thought you were only "quite pretty".'

'I have no interest in what Mr Darcy thinks,' Elizabeth answered, laughing. 'Mr Darcy is very rich and handsome, but he is also very proud. I will never like him!'

During the next month, the Bennets met their new neighbours several times. Jane and Bingley enjoyed being with each other more and more and Mrs Bennet was delighted.

Darcy was very surprised when he began to be interested in Elizabeth Bennet. Darcy disliked her family – he thought that Mrs Bennet and her youngest daughters were noisy and rude. But he admired Elizabeth's clever conversation and her beautiful dark eyes.

One evening, there was a party at Lucas Lodge, the home of Sir William and Lady Lucas, the Bennets' neighbours.

Elizabeth noticed that Mr Darcy, who was standing near her, was watching her closely.

'Why is he standing there, listening to every word I say?' Elizabeth whispered to her friend, Charlotte Lucas.

'That is a question only Mr Darcy can answer,' Charlotte replied.

'I am going to speak to him,' Elizabeth said. 'He is proud and cold. And I shall become afraid of him if I don't tease him a little.'

Elizabeth stood up and smiled at Darcy.

'You heard me asking Colonel Forster to arrange a ball in Meryton,' she said. 'Do you think I said the right things to him?'

'Yes, you did,' Mr Darcy answered. 'Young ladies always say the right things when they want to go to a ball.'

'You do not have a good opinion[23] of us,' Elizabeth replied.

At that moment, Mary Bennet sat down to play the piano. Mary was the only plain[24] girl in the Bennet family. She was quiet and liked to study. Soon Mary was asked to play some music for dancing.

Sir William Lucas called to Elizabeth. 'My dear Miss Elizabeth,

New Neighbours

you must dance! Here is Mr Darcy. He will be your partner, I am sure!'

Elizabeth expected[25] Mr Darcy to walk away. But, to her surprise, he bowed[26] politely.

'Will you dance with me, Miss Elizabeth?' he asked.

'I do not want to dance this evening,' Elizabeth said quickly. 'But thank you for asking me,' she said, as she turned away.

Miss Caroline Bingley had been watching them. She now walked up to Mr Darcy and smiled.

'I know what you are thinking, Mr Darcy,' she said. 'There is no one here who interests you this evening. You are as bored as I am.'

'You are wrong,' Darcy answered. 'I was thinking how attractive the fine eyes of a pretty woman can be.'

Miss Bingley thought that he was talking about her. She smiled happily.

'I was speaking about Miss Elizabeth Bennet,' Darcy said quietly.

'Miss Elizabeth Bennet?' Miss Bingley repeated in angry surprise. 'How long have you been interested in her? When can I congratulate you both on your engagement[27]?'

'That is exactly what I expected you to say,' Darcy replied. 'But one compliment[28] does not always lead to marriage.'

'You mentioned marriage!' Miss Bingley cried. 'What a delightful mother-in-law you will have! You must invite her to your house in Derbyshire. You will most certainly enjoy her visits to Pemberley!'

Mr Darcy did not reply. He listened calmly as Miss Bingley talked on. She soon decided that Darcy was not in love with Elizabeth Bennet.

Miss Bingley felt happier, because she planned to marry Mr Darcy herself!

2

Mrs Bennet's Plan

Mrs Phillips, Mrs Bennet's sister, lived in the town of Meryton, about a mile from Longbourn. Usually, Kitty and Lydia Bennet visited their aunt two or three times a week.

Now that the militia was in Meryton, the girls went there every day, hoping to meet the officers. Soon they talked only of handsome young men in red coats.

Mrs Bennet was happy that the girls went to Meryton to meet the officers. 'I liked talking to officers when I was a girl,' Mrs Bennet said. 'What a chance for Kitty or Lydia, Mr Bennet! If a young officer asked to marry one of them, I would not say no!'

The girls laughed and blushed.

'No one will ever want to marry such silly girls,' Mr Bennet told them severely.

One morning, a note arrived for Miss Jane Bennet.

'It is from Netherfield Hall – from Miss Bingley,' Jane said and read the note aloud.

My dear friend,

The gentlemen are dining with the officers today. Louisa and I will be alone here. Do come and have dinner with us, or we shall be so bored! Come as soon as you receive this note.

Yours ever,
Caroline Bingley

'I'm sorry the gentlemen are not having dinner at Netherfield,' Mrs Bennet said.

'Shall I go in the carriage?' Jane asked.

'No, no, my dear,' Mrs Bennet answered quickly. 'You must go on horseback. It's sure to rain. If you get wet, they will have to ask you to stay the night.'

Not long after Jane left, the rain began to fall heavily. Mrs Bennet was delighted when Jane did not return.

Just after breakfast the following morning, Jane sent Elizabeth a short note from Netherfield Hall.

My dear Lizzy,

I got very wet yesterday. I feel ill today and am staying in bed. My kind friends here have asked the doctor to come, but there is nothing much wrong with me except a headache.

Your loving sister,
Jane

'Well, Mrs Bennet,' her husband said, 'thanks to you, your daughter may become dangerously ill. But I suppose you think your idea was a good one.'

'Yes, I do. Jane won't die of a cold,' Mrs Bennet answered, laughing. 'While she stays there, she will get to know Mr Bingley better.'

'But Jane is ill,' Elizabeth said. 'I shall walk to Netherfield to see her.'

'Don't be silly,' her mother cried. 'Your clothes will get covered with mud. What will Miss Bingley think?'

'I don't care what she thinks,' Elizabeth replied. 'It is only three miles to Netherfield. I shall be back before dinner.'

'We will walk into Meryton with you,' Kitty and Lydia said together. They wanted to see the officers and gossip with their aunt.

Elizabeth left her sisters in Meryton and walked on alone. She walked quickly and cheerfully across the muddy fields. By the time she reached Netherfield, the bottom of her dress was very dirty. But her face was pink and her eyes were bright.

After speaking to the Bingleys, Elizabeth ran quickly upstairs to see Jane.

Caroline Bingley looked at her sister and they both laughed unkindly.

Mrs Bennet's Plan

'She walked three miles across the wet fields,' Caroline said. 'Did you see how untidy her hair was, Louisa?'

'Yes, I did. And did you see the mud on her dress?' Louisa replied.

'I thought Miss Elizabeth Bennet looked very pretty,' Mr Bingley said. 'I did not see the mud.'

'I'm sure you saw the mud on her clothes, Mr Darcy,' Caroline went on. 'I'm sure you would not let your sister, Georgiana, walk three miles across muddy fields!'

'Certainly not,' Darcy replied.

'Then do you still admire the lady's fine eyes?' Miss Bingley whispered.

'Yes, I do,' Darcy replied calmly. 'The exercise[29] made them brighter.'

At that moment, Elizabeth came back into the room. She said that Jane was no better.

'Then you must stay here with her,' Mr Bingley said kindly. 'Do not think of leaving Netherfield.'

'Thank you, I am very grateful,' Elizabeth replied. 'Jane is very ill. I think my mother should come and see her.'

Mr Bingley smiled.

'Of course Mrs Bennet must come,' he said. 'Write her a note and a servant will take it in the morning.'

As soon as Mrs Bennet received her daughter's note the next day, she went to Netherfield in her carriage. Kitty and Lydia, who wanted to see Mr Bingley again, went with her.

Mrs Bennet was delighted to see that Jane was still in bed. Mrs Bennet hurried to speak to Mr Bingley.

'I'm afraid that poor dear Jane is too ill to leave, Mr Bingley,' she told him.

'Leave? Certainly not, Mrs Bennet. My sister and I want Miss Bennet to stay until she is well,' Bingley replied.

'Oh, thank you!' Mrs Bennet cried. 'My dear Jane is very ill, but she does not complain! She is the most good-natured girl that I know.'

Mrs Bennet's Plan

As she was speaking, Mrs Bennet was looking around her with the greatest interest.

'This is a delightful room, Mr Bingley,' she said. 'Netherfield is a very fine house. I hope you are planning to stay here. A young man of your age should be settling down[30].'

'At present, I intend to stay,' Bingley replied. 'But whatever I do, I do in a hurry. If I change my mind[31], I shall leave quickly.'

'That is exactly what I thought,' Elizabeth said quietly.

'Then you understand me very well,' Bingley told Elizabeth smiling. 'You study people closely. That must be interesting for you.'

'Yes, it is,' Elizabeth replied. 'It is very interesting when their characters[32] are difficult to understand.'

She looked at Mr Darcy as she spoke. He smiled.

'You cannot have many chances to study people here – in the country,' Darcy said.

'Perhaps not. But even people we know well can surprise us. There is always something new to interest me,' Elizabeth replied.

'That is true,' Mrs Bennet said. 'There is always something happening in the country. I think the country is more interesting than London. But,' she went on, with an angry look at Mr Darcy, 'that gentleman does not think so.'

Elizabeth was upset by her mother's rudeness.

'Mother, you did not understand Mr Darcy,' she said quickly. 'He only meant that there are fewer people in the country.'

'But we know a great many people!' Mrs Bennet cried. 'I would like Mr Darcy to know that there are twenty-four families we know well!'

Mrs Bennet's foolish answer made Miss Bingley sigh. She looked across at Mr Darcy and smiled.

'The Lucases are our closest friends,' Mrs Bennet said. 'Sir William always has something pleasant to say to everyone.

'I'm sorry his daughter, Charlotte, is so plain,' Mrs Bennet went on. 'Lady Lucas has told me many times how much she admires my Jane's beauty!'

Mrs Bennet's Plan

There was silence and, soon afterwards, Mrs Bennet decided to leave. Then Lydia, who had been whispering and laughing with Kitty, spoke to Mr Bingley.

'When we were dancing in Meryton, you promised to give a ball,' Lydia said. 'I hope you haven't forgotten, Mr Bingley.'

'I certainly have not,' Mr Bingley replied. 'As soon as your sister is better, there will be a ball at Netherfield!'

When Mrs Bennet, Lydia and Kitty had left, Miss Bingley spoke to her brother. 'Are you going to have a ball here, Charles? Some of us don't like dancing.'

'If you mean Darcy, he can go to bed,' Bingley answered, laughing. 'But I am going to have a ball.'

Elizabeth stayed upstairs with Jane all day. Then, in the evening, she went to sit with the others downstairs.

Mr Darcy was writing a letter and Miss Bingley was sitting near him.

Elizabeth was amused by their conversation.

'Mr Darcy, Georgiana will be delighted to receive such a long letter!' Miss Bingley said. 'Do tell your sister that I am looking forward to[33] seeing her in January!'

'I have already done so. You asked me before.'

'Your writing is so clear, Mr Darcy,' Caroline Bingley went on. 'Charles writes so badly that he leaves out half the words!'

'I do – that is because I think so fast,' Bingley said.

'So you are proud of writing badly,' Darcy told him.

Bingley laughed.

'You see how Darcy always says something clever, Miss Bennet!' he said to Elizabeth. 'He is taller than me too, so I have to agree with him!'

Darcy smiled, but he said nothing more. Then Miss Bingley sat down to play the piano. Her sister, Louisa, began to sing.

Soon Elizabeth noticed that Mr Darcy was not looking at them. He was looking at her. Why? Was he interested in her?

Miss Bingley began to play music for dancing and Darcy stood up and walked towards Elizabeth.

'Doesn't this music make you want to dance, Miss Bennet?' he asked politely.

Elizabeth smiled, but did not answer. After a moment, Darcy repeated his question. Elizabeth looked up at him, her dark eyes sparkling with amusement.

'I heard your question,' she said, 'but I could not think of what to say.

'If I say yes,' she went on, 'you will think I am silly and foolish. You will think I am like other girls who are only interested in dancing. So, Mr Darcy, my answer is no, I do not wish to dance. Think I am silly and foolish if you dare[34].'

'Miss Bennet, I do not dare.'

Caroline Bingley saw them talking to each other and she was jealous. As soon as Elizabeth had gone upstairs to see Jane, Caroline spoke to Mr Darcy.

'When you are married, Mr Darcy, I hope you will teach the Bennet family some manners,' she said. 'You will have to stop Mrs Bennet chattering so much. And you will have to tell Kitty and Lydia to stop talking to the officers all the time!'

The next day, Jane felt better. After dinner, she went downstairs with Elizabeth. With a kind smile, Bingley led Jane to a chair near the fire. Bingley sat down beside her and they began talking quietly.

Darcy was reading and soon Miss Bingley picked up a book too.

'I love to read in the evening,' Miss Bingley said, looking at Darcy. 'I do enjoy reading!'

But a few minutes later, she stood up and began to walk around the room.

Mr Darcy went on reading and did not look up.

'Miss Elizabeth Bennet,' Miss Bingley called to Elizabeth. 'Come and walk with me!'

Elizabeth was surprised. But she stood up and began to walk with Miss Bingley.

Darcy looked up at once. Very soon, he closed his book.

'Oh, Mr Darcy, will you walk with us?' Miss Bingley asked. 'The exercise is so pleasant!'

'Thank you. But I don't think you want me to walk with you,' Darcy replied.

'What does Mr Darcy mean? Shall we ask him, Miss Elizabeth?' Miss Bingley said loudly.

'No,' Elizabeth replied. 'The best way to tease him is to ask him nothing.'

But Miss Bingley wanted an answer. 'What do you mean, Mr Darcy?' she asked.

'Very well, I will explain,' Mr Darcy said. 'There are two reasons why I don't think you want me to walk with you. Either you want to tell each other secrets. Or you know how attractive you look when you are walking. If the first reason is true, I would be in your way. If the second reason is true, I can admire you better from here.'

'Oh, Mr Darcy, you mustn't say such things!' said Miss Bingley. 'How shall we punish[35] him, Miss Elizabeth?'

'That's easy. Tease him. Laugh at him.' Elizabeth said.

Miss Bingley shook her head.

'We cannot tease Mr Darcy. No one dares to laugh at him.'

'Not laugh at him?' Elizabeth repeated. 'I dare to laugh at him. I love to laugh.'

Mr Darcy was quick to answer her.

'The wisest man can be made to look foolish,' he said.

'I never laugh at wise people or good people,' Elizabeth replied. 'But I like to study people's faults[36]. You, of course, Mr Darcy, have no faults at all.'

'Of course I have faults,' Darcy replied quickly. 'But I always try not to have faults that make me look foolish.'

'Do you mean faults like vanity and pride[37]?' Elizabeth asked quietly.

'I think vanity is a fault,' Darcy answered quickly. 'But pride is never a fault. It is not wrong to be proud of your family and your position in society[38].'

'Oh, Mr Darcy, will you walk with us?' Miss Bingley asked.
'The exercise is so pleasant!'

Elizabeth turned away so that Darcy would not see her smiling.

'What have you found out about Mr Darcy, Miss Elizabeth?' Miss Bingley called.

'I have found out that he has no faults. He is perfect.'

'No,' Darcy said seriously, 'that is not true. I'm not perfect, Miss Bennet. I know that I do not like people who are foolish or unkind. And I do not forgive anyone who has harmed me. Once I have an opinion of someone I never change my mind.'

'Then your fault is to see faults in everybody else,' Elizabeth replied.

'And your fault,' Darcy answered with a smile, 'is to enjoy not understanding people.'

Miss Bingley thought that Darcy and Elizabeth had talked for long enough.

'Please play the piano for us, Miss Elizabeth,' she called. So Elizabeth left Darcy and went to the piano.

The next day, Jane was better and the Bennet sisters decided to leave Netherfield. Bingley was sorry that Jane was leaving, but his sister, Caroline, was pleased that Elizabeth was leaving.

Mr Darcy was pleased too. He was beginning to fall in love with Elizabeth. But he decided that she must never know his feelings. Mr Fitzwilliam Darcy of Pemberley came from a rich and noble family. Miss Elizabeth Bennet had no chance of marrying him.

3

The Bennets Have a Visitor

At breakfast the following morning Mr Bennet had some very surprising news for everybody.

The Bennets Have a Visitor

'We must have something good to eat for dinner today, Mrs Bennet,' Mr Bennet said. 'I am expecting a visitor – a gentleman.'

'A gentleman?' Mrs Bennet repeated. 'It must be Mr Bingley. Jane, you silly girl, why didn't you tell me he was coming?'

'It is not Mr Bingley,' Mr Bennet replied. 'Our visitor is someone I have never seen before.

'A month ago, I had a letter from my cousin, Mr Collins. As you all know, Mr Collins will inherit[39] this house when I die. He can make you leave Longbourn House. He can live here himself if he wants to.'

'Don't talk about Mr Collins to me!' Mrs Bennet cried. 'I refuse to let him visit us!'

'Well, I have invited him,' Mr Bennet said. 'He wishes to be friends with us all. Mr Collins is a clergyman[40] and has the living at Hunsford, in Kent. He tells me that his patron is Lady Catherine de Bourgh and he says she is a very great lady.

'Mr Collins' letter is very long and what he says is not clear,' Mr Bennet went on. 'I think he is a very foolish young man. He will arrive this afternoon and he will be staying for twelve days.'

Mr Collins arrived at exactly four o'clock. He was a tall, fat young man. He was twenty-five, but he looked much older. Mr Collins was very polite to everyone.

'I must compliment you on the beauty of your daughters, Mrs Bennet,' he said. 'And I am sure that they are all looking forward to getting married. But I shall say more about marriage later.'

Next, Mr Collins complimented Mrs Bennet on the house and furniture. At dinner, he made compliments about the food. But his greatest compliments were about Lady Catherine de Bourgh, his noble patron[41].

'Lady Catherine de Bourgh behaves as every lady should behave,' Mr Collins said. 'She is proud, but she is most kind and helpful to people in lower positions in society. She has kindly invited me to her home, Rosings Park, many times.'

'Do you live near Rosings Park?' Mr Bennet asked.

'I can see Rosings from my own house,' Mr Collins replied,

smiling. 'Lady Catherine often stops her carriage and speaks to me. And I pay her compliments, as I think I should.

'Lady Catherine, my patron, gave me the living at Hunsford,' he went on. 'I have a good house and a good income[42]. Now I need a wife. Lady Catherine has told me that I must get married. My wife must respect[43] Lady Catherine, of course.'

As he spoke, Mr Collins smiled at each of the Bennet girls.

The following day, Mr Collins spoke to Mrs Bennet.

'I have come to Longbourn because I want a wife,' Mr Collins said. 'I have decided to choose your eldest daughter, Jane. I am sure Lady Catherine will agree with my choice.'

Mrs Bennet smiled.

'Jane is a beautiful girl, everyone says so. But I must tell you, Mr Collins, Jane will soon be engaged to be married. But our second child, our dear Elizabeth ...'

Mr Collins understood immediately.

'Then Miss Elizabeth will be my choice,' he said. 'I am sure Lady Catherine will be delighted with her.'

By the second day of the visit, Mr Bennet was very tired of Mr Collins. When the girls decided to walk into Meryton, Mr Bennet spoke quietly to Elizabeth.

'Do take Mr Collins with you,' Mr Bennet said. 'Every time I go into my library, he follows me there to talk about Lady Catherine de Bourgh. I don't want to listen to him! I want to be alone somewhere in the house.'

In Meryton, Kitty and Lydia were delighted to see Mr Denny, an officer they knew well. He bowed politely and introduced his friend – Mr George Wickham.

Mr Wickham, who had just joined the militia, was a handsome young man. He looked very smart in his red coat. The young men and women were soon chattering happily.

A few minutes later, they heard the sound of horses coming. Mr Darcy and Mr Bingley were riding towards them. The gentlemen

The Bennets Have a Visitor

stopped their horses. Mr Bingley spoke to everyone politely and then he began talking to Jane.

Elizabeth looked at Mr Darcy. She was surprised to see him staring at George Wickham. Darcy's face was pale with anger and Wickham's face was very red. The two men did not speak.

Soon afterwards, Darcy and Bingley rode away and the Bennet girls said goodbye to the officers. The girls walked on with Mr Collins to their Aunt Phillips' house. She was delighted to see them.

'Some officers are coming here for dinner tomorrow,' Mrs Phillips said. 'Why don't you all come here after dinner? We can have a game of cards, gossip and enjoy ourselves.'

Mrs Phillips promised Lydia that Mr George Wickham would be invited.

The girls arrived early the following evening. They were all looking forward to seeing Mr George Wickham again. When the

The Bennets Have a Visitor

gentlemen came in, Mr Wickham looked round the room and smiled at everyone. He sat down beside Elizabeth Bennet.

They talked for a few minutes and then Mr Wickham said, 'I believe that the two gentlemen we saw yesterday are staying at Netherfield Hall. Is Netherfield Hall far from Meryton?'

'About two miles away,' Elizabeth replied.

'And how long has Mr Darcy been staying there?' Wickham asked.

'For more than a month,' Elizabeth answered. 'Have you met him before, Mr Wickham? I have heard that Mr Darcy has a large house in Derbyshire. Is that true?'

'Yes, Pemberley is a very fine house,' Mr Wickham replied. 'The estate is very large too. I know the house and family very well. Do you know Mr Darcy well, Miss Bennet?'

'Yes, I know him as well as I want to know him,' Elizabeth replied sharply. 'I stayed at Netherfield for four days. That was a long time to be in the same house as Mr Darcy!'

Wickham smiled.

'I can understand that,' he said.

'The people of Meryton are not good enough for Mr Darcy,' Elizabeth went on. 'He is not liked here. His pride has made people dislike him.'

'I am not surprised that people do not like him,' Wickham answered, 'Many people like Mr Darcy at first. They know that he comes from a noble family and is very rich. Then they find out that he is very proud. I hope he does not plan to stay in the neighbourhood much longer. But if he does, he won't make me leave!'

Elizabeth was surprised by Mr Wickham's words.

'Has Mr Darcy harmed you in any way?' she asked quietly.

'Let me explain,' Wickham answered. He waited for a moment and then went on.

'I shall enjoy being in the militia,' he said, 'but I had planned a very different life for myself. I was going to become a clergyman, but Mr Darcy stopped me.'

'He stopped you becoming a clergyman? I do not understand.'

The Bennets Have a Visitor

'My father was steward[44] of the Pemberley estate,' Wickham went on. 'Old Mr Darcy – Mr Darcy's father - was very good to me. He promised me the living at Pemberley. But then he died.'

Wickham sighed.

'Mr Fitzwilliam Darcy refused to do what his father wanted. He would not give me the living at Pemberley. Mr Darcy has been kind and helpful to some people, but not to me. He does not wish to help me. I used to know Darcy's sister, Georgiana, very well. But she is proud, like her brother.'

Elizabeth believed everything that Mr Wickham told her. She had understood Mr Darcy's character well! He had behaved badly towards George Wickham. But something was worrying her.

'Mr Bingley is a very pleasant, good-natured man,' she said. 'Does he know what Mr Darcy did to you?'

'I don't think he does. People see that Mr Darcy is noble and has good manners. They do not understand that he is hard and unkind. But I know him too well.'

Later in the evening, Mr Wickham heard Mr Collins talking about Lady Catherine de Bourgh.

'Does Mr Collins know the de Bourgh family well?' Wickham whispered to Elizabeth. 'Lady Catherine is Mr Darcy's aunt. She expects him to marry her daughter, Anne de Bourgh.'

Elizabeth smiled. Poor Miss Bingley! She had no chance of becoming Mr Darcy's wife!

On the way home, Elizabeth thought about what Wickham had told her. When Elizabeth was alone with Jane, she told her everything.

'Mr Wickham's story can't be true!' Jane said. 'Is Mr Darcy so very bad? Why is Mr Bingley his friend? I do not know what to think.'

Elizabeth laughed.

'You are too kind, Jane,' she said. 'You want everyone to be good-natured like you. I know what I think!

'Mr Darcy is a proud man – he has told me so himself. He does not care about anyone who is in a lower position in society. He has behaved badly towards George Wickham. Mr Wickham is right to be angry.'

A few days later, Mr Bingley and his sisters called at Longbourn House. Everyone was invited to a ball at Netherfield Hall on the following Tuesday.

Rain fell heavily for the next four days. The girls could not walk into Meryton and gossip with Aunt Phillips. But the Bennet girls were happy. They were looking forward to the Netherfield Ball.

4

The Netherfield Ball

Elizabeth was happy and excited as she got dressed for the ball. She knew that Mr Wickham admired her and she wanted to look beautiful.

When the Bennet girls arrived at Netherfield Hall, Lydia looked for Mr Wickham. She ran across the room to where some officers were standing.

'Oh, Mr Denny,' Lydia cried, 'where is Mr Wickham?'

'He is in London,' Mr Denny replied. Then, he saw Elizabeth and he went on, 'I think Wickham did not want to meet Mr Darcy.'

Elizabeth was very disappointed that Wickham was not there. When Mr Darcy spoke to her politely, Elizabeth was angry and did not want to speak to him. But she could not be angry for long and she made up her mind to enjoy herself.

Unfortunately, Mr Collins had chosen Elizabeth to be his first dancing partner. Mr Collins was a very bad dancer. Elizabeth was very glad when the dance ended.

Her next partner was an officer. Elizabeth smiled when he told her how much everyone liked George Wickham.

The Netherfield Ball

Later, as Elizabeth was talking to Charlotte Lucas, she saw Mr Darcy coming towards them. When he asked Elizabeth to dance with him, she was so surprised that she agreed.

When the dance began, Elizabeth and Darcy stood opposite each other without speaking. Then Elizabeth asked a question and Darcy answered. After a short silence, Elizabeth spoke again.

'It is your turn to say something now, Mr Darcy,' she said.

Mr Darcy smiled.

'I am happy to say anything you want me to say, Miss Bennet,' he said.

'Good, you have said enough. Now we can be silent for a time. Then I shall speak and you must answer.'

'Are these rules to please you or to please me?' Darcy asked.

'Both,' Elizabeth replied, smiling.

It was Mr Darcy who spoke next.

'I believe you and your sisters often walk into Meryton,' he said.

'Yes, we do,' Elizabeth replied. 'When you saw us there the other day, we were talking to a new friend of ours – Mr George Wickham.'

Darcy looked angry.

'Mr Wickham makes friends easily,' Darcy said in a cold voice. 'But he often loses them.'

'He has lost your friendship,' Elizabeth replied sharply. 'He may never succeed in life now.'

Darcy was silent and the dance continued. A few moments later, Sir William Lucas came up. He bowed to them and said, 'It is good to see you dancing, my dear sir. Miss Elizabeth Bennet is a delightful partner. I'm sure we will all have many pleasant evenings here – especially after a certain event[45] takes place.'

Sir William looked at Jane and Bingley, who were dancing together. 'We shall soon be congratulating our young friends,' he said.

Darcy was very surprised by these words. He looked quickly at Bingley and Jane. Then he looked back at Elizabeth.

The Netherfield Ball

'I'm sorry. I have forgotten what we were talking about,' Darcy said.

'I do not think we were talking at all,' Elizabeth replied. 'We seem to have very little to say to each other.'

'Perhaps we can talk about books,' Darcy said, smiling.

'I cannot talk about books in a ballroom,' Elizabeth answered.

'Mr Darcy,' she went on, 'you once said that you did not forgive people who had harmed you. I hope you think carefully before you make up your mind to dislike someone.'

'I do,' Darcy said.

'And you are never prejudiced[46]?'

'I hope not.'

'Then you must always believe that you are right,' Elizabeth said quietly.

'Why you are asking me all these questions, Miss Bennet?' Darcy asked.

'So that I can understand your character, Mr Darcy. People have so many different opinions of you that I do not know what to think.'

'Perhaps you should learn more about me before you decide that you understand me,' Darcy replied seriously.

'But I may not meet you again,' replied Elizabeth, smiling. 'I may not have another chance to understand you.'

'Then you must do what pleases you,' said Darcy coldly.

They finished the dance without speaking again. They were both unhappy. But Darcy could forgive Elizabeth because he was falling in love with her.

As soon as Elizabeth was alone, Miss Bingley walked up to her.

'So, Miss Elizabeth, you are now interested in Mr George Wickham,' Miss Bingley said. 'Your sister, Lydia, has been asking a thousand questions about him. I believe that Mr Wickham has not told you the truth about himself and Mr Darcy. Mr Wickham does not always tell the truth. He is the son of a steward, Miss Elizabeth!'

'Mr Wickham told me that himself,' Elizabeth replied angrily.

The Netherfield Ball

'Did he? I'm sorry. I was only trying to help you,' Miss Bingley said as she walked away.

What a rude girl, Elizabeth thought. She will not make me change my mind about Wickham and Darcy.

Then Elizabeth went to speak to Jane. 'I came to ask what you found out about Mr Wickham,' Elizabeth said. 'But I can see that you and Mr Bingley are only interested in each other.'

Jane blushed, then she said, 'Mr Bingley told me that Mr Darcy has always behaved well towards Mr Wickham. But Mr Wickham has behaved badly.'

'Does Mr Bingley know Mr Wickham?' Elizabeth asked.

'He met him for the first time in Meryton, the other day,' Jane replied.

'Then Mr Bingley does not know the truth. He does not know what Mr Darcy did to Mr Wickham,' Elizabeth said sharply. 'I thought Mr Darcy was proud and unkind when I first met him. Now I know that I was right.'

At that moment, Mr Collins came up. He was very excited.

'I have discovered that a relation of my patron, Lady Catherine de Bourgh, is here tonight. Mr Darcy is her nephew! I must speak to him at once,' Mr Collins said.

Elizabeth was embarrassed[47] by Mr Collins' foolishness. She watched him make a low bow to Mr Darcy and begin to speak to him.

Later, at supper, Elizabeth sat near her mother. Mrs Bennet was talking to Lady Lucas in a very loud voice. Mr Darcy was sitting opposite them, and he could hear every word she said.

'Well, Lady Lucas,' Mrs Bennet said happily, 'I hope you are going to congratulate me. Jane will soon be married and living here at Netherfield with Mr Bingley! He is so delightful – and so very rich! And my other daughters will all meet rich young men too! We may even find a husband for your daughter Charlotte, Lady Lucas.'

'Please speak more quietly,' Elizabeth whispered to her mother. 'Mr Darcy can hear every word you say!'

The Netherfield Ball

'What do I care about Mr Darcy?' Mrs Bennet cried in a loud voice.

'Please don't shout!' Elizabeth said, embarrassed at her mother's rudeness. 'Mr Darcy is Mr Bingley's friend. You must be polite to him.'

But nothing could stop Mrs Bennet talking about Jane and Bingley's marriage. Mr Darcy looked more and more serious. He did not think his friend, Charles Bingley of Netherfield Hall, should marry Miss Jane Bennet.

After supper, the young ladies were asked to sing. Mary Bennet was the first person to do so. Her voice was not good, but she was very proud of it. As Mary began her second song, Bingley's sisters began to laugh. Elizabeth quietly asked her father to stop Mary singing at once.

'That is enough, Mary my child,' Mr Bennet said. 'Let some other young lady sing to us now!'

Elizabeth became more and more unhappy as the evening went on. Mr Collins asked her to dance with him again. When Elizabeth refused, Mr Collins went on talking to her, so that she could not dance with anyone else. Elizabeth was becoming worried about Mr Collins. Was he thinking of marrying her?

The Bennets were the last family to leave Netherfield that evening because Mrs Bennet wanted Jane to spend more time with Bingley. Bingley's sisters were tired and they were pleased when their guests left at last.

Before Mrs Bennet left, she invited Mr Bingley to have dinner with them very soon. Bingley said that he had to go to London the following day. But when he returned, he would be happy to have dinner at Longbourn. Mrs Bennet was pleased. She was sure that Jane would soon be married to Mr Charles Bingley.

5

Mr Collins Finds a Wife

The next day, Mr Collins decided to propose[48] to Elizabeth. After breakfast, he found Mrs Bennet, Elizabeth and Kitty sitting together.

'May I speak to your daughter Elizabeth alone, madam?' Mr Collins asked Mrs Bennet politely.

'Oh, my dear sir! Yes, of course,' Mrs Bennet said. 'I am sure Elizabeth will be pleased. Come along, Kitty, I want to speak to you upstairs.'

'Please do not go!' Elizabeth cried as she stood up. 'I am sure Mr Collins has nothing important to say.'

'Lizzy, I want you to stay here!' Mrs Bennet said. 'Lizzy, you must stay and listen to Mr Collins!'

Elizabeth sighed and sat down again. As soon as they were alone, Mr Collins began speaking.

'My dear Miss Elizabeth, I am sure that you know of my feelings. As soon as I saw you, I chose you to be my wife. I have made a good choice, I am sure.

'Let me explain why I wish to marry,' he went on. Firstly, I think that all clergymen should be married. Secondly, marriage will make me happier. And thirdly – and most importantly – I have been told to marry by my patron, Lady Catherine de Bourgh. Lady Catherine has promised to visit my wife often. With Lady Catherine as our patron, we will be very happy.

'As you know, I will inherit this estate when your father dies. So, if I marry one of his daughters, I will be helping you all. You have very little money, but that is not important. My own income is good. In fact, our marriage will please everyone.'

'Please stop a minute!' Elizabeth cried. 'Marriage to you will not please me. I am grateful for your proposal, but I must refuse.'

Mr Collins laughed and shook his head.

'I understand,' he said. 'Young ladies always refuse proposals of marriage at first. They begin by saying no, but they mean yes!'

'I am not one of those young ladies,' Elizabeth said. 'You could never make me happy. Also, I am sure I could never please you – or Lady Catherine!'

'Lady Catherine will enjoy your clever conversation,' Mr Collins said. 'But I am sure you will show her respect. When I next see her, I will tell Lady Catherine that you will be an excellent wife for me.'

'You do not need to tell her this,' Elizabeth replied, 'because I do not want to be your wife.'

'I cannot believe that,' Mr Collins said, smiling. 'I have a good house and a good income. You are not rich – you may never receive another proposal. You cannot refuse mine.'

'You are wrong, sir,' Elizabeth said, as she turned to leave the room. 'I am refusing your proposal of marriage.'

'You are delightful!' Mr Collins cried. 'But I know your parents will want you to accept my proposal. You will not be allowed to say no!'

Mr Collins Finds a Wife

Elizabeth left the room without speaking. She ran quickly upstairs. A few minutes later, Mrs Bennet came in. She smiled and congratulated Mr Collins. But when he told her Elizabeth's answer, Mrs Bennet was very unhappy.

'Elizabeth must accept your proposal,' Mrs Bennet said. 'She is a silly, thoughtless girl!'

Mr Collins began to look worried.

'Oh, Mrs Bennet,' he said. 'Silly and thoughtless? Perhaps Elizabeth will not be a good wife for me.'

Mrs Bennet was worried now.

'Sir, you do not understand me,' she said. 'Lizzy is a very good-natured girl. I will go to Mr Bennet and he will talk to her.'

Mrs Bennet ran to the library.

'Oh, Mr Bennet!' she cried. 'Lizzy has refused Mr Collins' proposal. You must make her marry him.'

Mr Bennet stopped reading his book.

'I do not understand, Mrs Bennet. What are you talking about?'

'I am talking about Mr Collins and Lizzy. Lizzy says she will not marry Mr Collins. Now I think Mr Collins does not want Lizzy. You must tell Lizzy to marry him!'

'I understand, Mrs Bennet,' said Mr Bennet calmly. 'Call Lizzy to the library. I shall give her my opinion.'

Elizabeth came into the library.

'Lizzy,' said her father. 'I have been told that Mr Collins has proposed to you. Is it true?'

'Yes, sir.'

'I understand. And you have refused his proposal?'

'I have, sir.'

'Then there is a problem. Your mother says that you must accept Mr Collins. That's right, isn't it, Mrs Bennet?'

'Yes, or I will refuse to see her again,' Mrs Bennet answered angrily.

'You have a difficult decision to make, Elizabeth,' Mr Bennet said. 'You are going to lose one of your parents. Your mother will refuse to see you again if you do not marry Mr Collins. And I will refuse to see you again if you do! And now, I want to read my book quietly, Mrs Bennet.'

Mrs Bennet was very disappointed. She tried to make Elizabeth change her mind, but she did not succeed.

Mr Collins decided that Elizabeth would not be a good wife for him. He sat alone and thought.

Not long afterwards, Charlotte Lucas came to Longbourn House. Lydia was the first to tell her the news about Mr Collins and Elizabeth. Mr Collins did not speak to Elizabeth again. He talked to Charlotte Lucas for the rest of the day.

After breakfast the next day, the girls walked to Meryton. They wanted to find out if Mr Wickham had returned. They were delighted to meet him in the town and he went with them to Mrs Phillips' house.

Mr Wickham told Elizabeth why he had not been at the Netherfield Ball.

'I decided that I did not want to meet Mr Darcy. I did not want to be in the same room as him.'

Wickham and another officer walked back to Longbourn with the girls and Elizabeth introduced Mr Wickham to her father and mother. Soon afterwards, Jane Bennet received a letter. Jane read it quickly and put it away. When their visitors had left, Elizabeth followed Jane upstairs to their room.

'Elizabeth, this letter is from Caroline Bingley,' Jane said. 'I am very surprised. Everyone has left Netherfield and they are on their way to London now. They are not going to return to Netherfield. I will read what Caroline has written.

'. . . We have decided to go with Charles to London. We shall stay at Mr Hurst's house in Grosvenor Street. I am sorry to leave you, my dear friend. I hope we will meet sometime in the future. I hope you will write to me ...'

Elizabeth was surprised, but she spoke cheerfully.

'Caroline wants to stay in London, but perhaps her brother will come back soon,' Elizabeth told her sister.

Jane shook her head sadly.

'Caroline writes that Mr Bingley will not be returning to Hertfordshire this winter. Listen,' she said.

'. . . *Charles has business in London and he will stay in London for some time. Many of our friends are already here. I hope, my dear friend, that your Christmas in Hertfordshire will be pleasant. I am sure you will be too busy and happy to miss us! ...* '

'I believe that Miss Bingley wants to keep you and her brother apart, but I do not think that she will succeed.' Elizabeth said angrily.

Jane looked at her sister. Her eyes were full of tears.

'You have not heard the end of the letter,' she said sadly. 'Miss Bingley goes on to say this:

' . . . *Mr Darcy is looking forward to seeing his sister again soon and so am I. Miss Georgiana Darcy is very beautiful! Louisa and I hope that one day she will marry Charles. Charles admires her very much and her family also wants them to get married. The marriage will bring much happiness to us all ...*'

'I understand now,' Jane said sadly. 'Caroline does not want me to marry her brother. And she is telling me too that Bingley does not want to marry me.'

'I do not agree,' Elizabeth said. 'I believe Miss Bingley knows that her brother is in love with you. But she wants him to marry Miss Darcy. So Caroline has followed Bingley to London because she wants to make him stay there.'

Jane did not answer.

'You must believe me, Jane!' Elizabeth cried. 'Everyone has seen you and Bingley together. They know that he loves you. But the Bennets are not rich or important like the Bingleys or the Darcys. And Caroline hopes to marry Mr Darcy herself.'

'I cannot believe that Caroline Bingley is so cruel,' Jane said

Mr Collins Finds a Wife

slowly. 'But could I ever marry a man whose sisters and friends were against me?'

'You must decide that for yourself,' Elizabeth said. 'If Miss Bingley's happiness is more important than your own happiness – then refuse to marry her brother!'

'Oh, Elizabeth!' Jane said, smiling. 'If Mr Bingley asked me to marry him I would accept his proposal immediately. But if he does not return to Netherfield this winter, he may never ask me. A lot can happen in six months!'

But Elizabeth told Jane to go on hoping that Mr Bingley would return. Then they went to tell Mrs Bennet that the Bingleys had left Netherfield for a short time. They did not tell her about Caroline Bingley's letter.

Later that day, the Bennets and Mr Collins dined with the Lucases. Charlotte Lucas sat next to Mr Collins. She agreed with everything he said. By the end of the evening, Charlotte's plan had succeeded. Mr Collins was interested in her.

The following morning, Mr Collins left Longbourn House very early. He hurried to Lucas Lodge. Charlotte was looking out of an upstairs window. She left the house immediately and went to meet Mr Collins. Mr Collins asked her to marry him and Charlotte accepted at once. Sir William and Lady Lucas were delighted with the news. Charlotte Lucas was twenty-seven and she was not very pretty. Charlotte was not in love with Mr Collins, but she had always planned to get married.

When Mr Collins returned to Longbourn House, he did not tell anyone what had happened.

The following morning Mr Collins went home. Before he left, he told the Bennets that he was going to return to Longbourn soon. Mrs Bennet hoped that he might marry one of her younger daughters – Mary, perhaps.

But after Mr Collins had left, Charlotte called at Longbourn to give Elizabeth her news.

'You are engaged to Mr Collins? My dear Charlotte, that is impossible!' Elizabeth cried.

'I understand that you are surprised, my dear Lizzy. I know Mr Collins proposed to you,' Charlotte replied calmly. 'I do not expect love. All I want is a home of my own. I think I can be happy with Mr Collins.'

At first, Mrs Bennet did not believe Charlotte's news. At last, Sir William told Mrs Bennet himself. She was very upset. She did not speak to the Lucases for a month.

'It is very hard, Mr Bennet,' Mrs Bennet said to her husband. 'When you die, Mr Bennet, Charlotte Lucas and Mr Collins will inherit this house. And I will have to leave. What a terrible thing to happen!'

'Then let us hope, my dear, that I live longer than you,' Mr Bennet answered.

Mr Collins soon returned to Longbourn and plans were made for his wedding. Charlotte did not want a long engagement. The wedding took place just before Christmas. Charlotte spoke quietly to Elizabeth before she left for Hunsford with Mr Collins.

'I hope you will write to me, Lizzy,' Charlotte said to her friend.

'Of course I shall write,' Elizabeth replied, 'and you must write to me too.'

'My father and sister are coming to Hunsford in March,' Charlotte went on. 'Promise me that you will come with them, Lizzy.'

Elizabeth agreed. But she did not think she would enjoy the visit.

6

Jane Loses All Hope

Jane answered Caroline Bingley's letter and waited anxiously[49] for a reply. Days went by, but Caroline did not write. People in Meryton said that Bingley would not return to Netherfield that

Jane Loses All Hope

winter. Mrs Bennet was very angry and she told everyone that Mr Bingley would return.

Elizabeth was worried. She began to think that Bingley's sisters and Mr Darcy were stopping Mr Bingley from meeting Jane again. Elizabeth felt sorry for her sister, because she knew that Jane still loved Bingley.

Then, at last, a letter arrived from Miss Bingley. The letter said that the Bingleys were all going to spend the winter in London. Mr Bingley was sorry that he had not said goodbye to his friends in Hertfordshire. He was now living in Mr Darcy's house in London. The rest of the letter was about Caroline's friendship with Georgiana Darcy.

Elizabeth was angry with Bingley. Had he listened to his sisters and Mr Darcy?

'I do not blame[50] Mr Bingley,' Jane said sadly. 'My unhappiness will not last for ever, but I will never forget him. He is the most pleasant and friendly young man I have ever met. But I was wrong to think he admired me.'

'My dear Jane,' Elizabeth said. 'You are too good-natured. I am finding it more and more difficult to understand people's behaviour. You are the only person I do understand, my dear sister. But people should take the blame when they make someone unhappy.'

'Please do not blame Mr Bingley,' Jane said. 'It was my vanity that made me think that he loved me.'

'Mr Bingley is thoughtless and weak,' Elizabeth replied. 'He has allowed his sisters and Mr Darcy to change his mind.'

'Perhaps they did not believe he loved me,' Jane answered. 'If they knew the truth, they would not be so unkind.'

Elizabeth did not speak of Mr Bingley again. But Mrs Bennet continued to complain that he had not returned to Netherfield Hall. At last, Elizabeth told her mother that she did not believe Bingley had loved Jane.

Mr Bennet was amused. 'Well, Lizzy,' he said to Elizabeth one day, 'your sister, Jane, has been disappointed in love. When will it

Jane Loses All Hope

be your turn, Lizzy? There are plenty of young officers to choose from. Mr Wickham perhaps? He is a pleasant young man – you could easily fall in love with him!'

Mr Wickham often came to Longbourn House. He had told his story about Mr Darcy to everyone in Meryton. And everyone but Jane believed Wickham's story. She refused to think badly of Darcy and nothing would make her change her mind.

It was Christmas. Mr Gardiner, Mrs Bennet's brother, arrived from London with his wife and children, to spend the holiday at Longbourn House.

Mr Gardiner had good manners and he was well-educated. His wife, who was several years younger than Mrs Bennet, was an intelligent and well-dressed woman. She cared very much for Jane and Elizabeth and they often stayed with her in London.

'We have had a difficult time here, sister,' Mrs Bennet told Mrs Gardiner. 'Two of our girls were nearly married, but everything went wrong.

'I do not blame Jane,' Mrs Bennet went on. 'She would have married Mr Bingley if she could. But Mr Collins proposed to Lizzy here in this room and she refused him. Charlotte Lucas married him instead. So now Lady Lucas has a married daughter and I haven't. It has all made me very anxious and ill. I am so pleased to have you here with us, sister.'

Later, when Mrs Gardiner was alone with Elizabeth, they talked about what had happened.

'I do feel sorry for Jane,' Mrs Gardiner said. 'Pleasant young men often fall in love with a pretty girl for a few weeks. But if he goes away the young man soon forgets the girl.'

'But Mr Bingley was in love with Jane. Every time they met, it became more clear that he was in love with her,' Elizabeth said. 'He danced with no one else. He did not answer when people spoke to him. These are signs of love, surely?'

'Yes. But he only loved her while he was here,' Mrs Gardiner

Jane Loses All Hope

said. 'Poor Jane! She may be unhappy for some time.

'But I have an idea, Lizzy,' Mrs Gardiner went on. 'I think I shall take Jane back to London with us after Christmas. What do you think?'

'I am sure that a visit to London will be good for her,' Elizabeth replied.

'But Jane must not hope to meet Mr Bingley,' Mrs Gardiner said. 'The Bingleys live in a fashionable part of London. Jane will never see Mr Bingley, unless he decides to call on us.'

'My dear aunt, that will never happen! Mr Darcy will not allow Mr Bingley to visit Jane,' Elizabeth replied.

Jane was very pleased when her aunt invited her to go to London. She hoped that Bingley's sisters would call on her while she was there.

The Gardiners stayed in Longbourn for a week. The officers from the militia were invited to Longbourn House several times and Mr Wickham was always with them. Mrs Gardiner enjoyed talking to George Wickham. Before her marriage, she had lived near Pemberley. She was interested to hear about Mr Darcy's behaviour to Wickham.

'Mr Wickham is a very pleasant young man, Lizzy, but you must not fall in love with him,' Mrs Gardiner said to her niece. 'He has no money. You must make a sensible marriage[51], Lizzy. Your father hopes and expects that you will marry sensibly.'

'These are serious words,' Elizabeth replied, smiling. 'At the moment, I am not in love with Mr Wickham. But I do enjoy being with him. I do not blame him for having no money. I blame Mr Darcy for that.

'I know my father likes Mr Wickham and young people often marry without much money. But I promise you, I will try not to fall in love with Mr Wickham!'

Mrs Gardiner laughed.

———

After Christmas, Jane and the Gardiners left Longbourn and went

Jane Loses All Hope

to London. Jane wrote to Miss Bingley at once and told her the Gardiners' address. After a week, Jane decided to call on Caroline Bingley.

Jane wrote to Elizabeth and told her about the visit.

... Caroline seemed pleased to see me. She didn't know I was in London. As I thought, she hadn't received my last letter. I asked her about Bingley, of course. Caroline told me that Bingley was always with Mr Darcy and she did not often see him. Miss Darcy was going to have dinner with them that day. I did not stay long, because Caroline and her sister were going out. I am sure they will return my call ...

Elizabeth read the letter carefully. She hoped that Mr Bingley would find out that Jane was in London. Elizabeth hoped that he would call on her sister!

Two weeks passed and then Jane wrote to Elizabeth again.

My dearest Lizzy,

You were right. Miss Bingley does not want to be my friend. She did not return my call until yesterday. She stayed only a short time and said nothing about seeing me again. But she spoke a lot about Miss Darcy. I must forget them all, Lizzy. Please write to me soon. I am sure that Mr Bingley knows I am in London. Miss Bingley has said that the Bingleys and Mr Darcy are not going to return to Netherfield.

I hope you will visit Charlotte in the spring. I am sure you will enjoy your stay at Hunsford ...

Then Elizabeth found out that Mr George Wickham was not interested in her any more. He now admired a Miss King, who had just inherited £10 000. She wrote to her aunt, Mrs Gardiner.

... I do not hate him or Miss King. I was never very much in love with Mr Wickham. Kitty and Lydia are more upset than I am. I know that even handsome young men need money ! ...

7
Elizabeth Visits Hunsford

The months of January and February passed slowly. In March, Elizabeth went to visit Charlotte and Mr Collins at Hunsford in Kent. She went with Sir William Lucas and Charlotte's younger sister, Maria.

On their way to Hunsford, Elizabeth and the Lucases went to see Jane in London and spend a night with the Gardiners there. They reached the Gardiners' house at midday. The rest of the day passed pleasantly and they went to the theatre in the evening. Mrs Gardiner told Elizabeth that Jane was often sad and quiet. Jane now believed that she would never see Bingley again.

'But what about you, my dear Lizzy?' Mrs Gardiner asked. 'Are you upset by Wickham's interest in Miss King? I hope Wickham is not thinking only of the young lady's money.

'But I have something more pleasant for you to think about, Lizzy,' Mrs Gardiner went on. 'Mr Gardiner and I are hoping to go to the Lake District[52] in the summer. Would you like to go with us, Lizzy?'

'My dear, dear aunt!' Elizabeth cried. 'That will be delightful. I shall look forward to it! There's no need to think about love and marriage when there are rocks and mountains to see! How I shall enjoy myself! And how I shall enjoy talking about everything when we return!'

Elizabeth thought about her holiday in the Lake District as she travelled to Hunsford with Sir William and Maria. At last, they could see Rosings Park and then Mr Collins' house. There was a garden in front of the house. And Mr and Mrs Collins were in the garden, smiling and waving at them.

Mr Collins showed them the house and then showed them the

garden. Mr Collins liked gardening and he wanted everybody to admire his garden. Then Mr Collins pointed towards Rosings which was nearby.

'I am happy to tell you, Miss Elizabeth, that Lady Catherine is at Rosings at present,' he said. 'We shall all have the pleasure of seeing her in church on Sunday. Charlotte and I have dinner at Rosings twice a week. Of course, while you are here, you will be invited to dinner too.'

The following afternoon, Miss de Bourgh, Lady Catherine's daughter, stopped her carriage in the lane outside Mr Collins' house. Charlotte and Mr Collins hurried out to talk to her.

'So that is Miss de Bourgh,' Elizabeth said to herself. 'How thin and small she is! She will be an excellent wife for Mr Darcy. Yes, she will be the best wife for him!'

Charlotte told Elizabeth and the Lucases that they were all invited to dinner at Rosings the next day.

'Do not worry about what to wear, my dear cousin,' Mr Collins told Elizabeth. 'Put on your best dress. Lady Catherine will not expect you to be as well-dressed as Miss de Bourgh.'

As the weather was good, they all walked across the park to Rosings.

Lady Catherine de Bourgh was a tall, large woman. Perhaps she had once been good-looking. She spoke to them all in a loud, clear voice. She stared hard at Mr Collins' visitors. Miss de Bourgh was not like her mother. She was pale and small and she did not say very much.

The dinner was very good. Mr Collins and Sir William complimented Lady Catherine on everything. Lady Catherine smiled at them.

After dinner, the ladies sat and listened to Lady Catherine. She gave Charlotte a lot of advice and asked Elizabeth questions about her family. Elizabeth thought that Lady Catherine was very rude, but she answered Lady Catherine's questions calmly.

'You are a young woman, but you give your opinions clearly,' Lady Catherine said. 'How old are you?

Elizabeth Visits Hunsford

'I have three younger sisters who are all grown up,' Elizabeth answered, smiling. 'So you cannot expect me to tell you.'

Lady Catherine looked very surprised at this answer.

'You cannot be more than twenty, I am sure,' Lady Catherine said.

'I am not yet twenty-one,' Elizabeth answered quietly.

After a week, Sir William went home. Elizabeth and Maria stayed at Hunsford. Mr Collins walked to Rosings nearly every day and Charlotte often went with him. Sometimes Lady Catherine called on the Collinses and gave them more advice. And they had dinner at Rosings several times.

Soon it was Easter. One evening, Lady Catherine said that her nephews, Mr Darcy and Colonel Fitzwilliam, were coming to stay at Rosings. Lady Catherine spoke well of Darcy. She was surprised that Charlotte and Elizabeth had already met him several times.

The morning after the gentlemen arrived, Mr Collins went to Rosings to call on Mr Darcy. When Mr Collins returned home, Mr Darcy and Colonel Fitzwilliam were with him.

Colonel Fitzwilliam was a pleasant man with fine manners and he talked politely for some time, but Mr Darcy sat quietly without speaking. At last, he asked Elizabeth about her family. Elizabeth answered him and then went on, 'My eldest sister has been in London for the past three months. Have you seen her there?'

Elizabeth thought that Mr Darcy looked a little embarrassed when she said this. But he told her that he had not seen Miss Jane Bennet.

A week passed before Lady Catherine invited Mr and Mrs Collins and their visitors to Rosings again. They were told to come after dinner, on the Sunday evening. Colonel Fitzwilliam sat beside Elizabeth and enjoyed her clever and intelligent conversation very much. Mr Darcy looked towards Elizabeth and Colonel Fitzwilliam so many times that Lady Catherine began to notice.

Elizabeth Visits Hunsford

'What are you talking about, Fitzwilliam?' she called. 'What are you telling Miss Bennet? Let me hear what you are saying!'

'We are talking about music, madam,' Fitzwilliam answered politely.

'Music!' Lady Catherine cried. 'Then let us all hear you. It is one of my favourite subjects. I am sure that my daughter would have been an excellent musician. But she has poor health and did not learn to play.'

Then Colonel Fitzwilliam asked Elizabeth to play the piano.

Lady Catherine went on talking to Darcy in a loud voice. But, after a time, he walked away from her to sit nearer the piano.

Elizabeth Visits Hunsford

When Elizabeth had finished playing, she turned to Darcy and smiled. 'You cannot frighten me by watching me so carefully, Mr Darcy.'

'You do not believe that I want to frighten you,' Mr Darcy replied. 'It amuses you to say things you do not believe!'

Elizabeth laughed and looked at Colonel Fitzwilliam.

'Mr Darcy wants to make you think badly of me,' she said. 'But you must be careful,' she went on, turning to Darcy. 'I may start telling the truth about you!'

'I am not afraid of that,' Darcy replied smiling.

'Let me hear what Darcy has done,' Colonel Fitzwilliam said to Elizabeth.

'The first time I saw Mr Darcy was at a ball,' Elizabeth replied. 'And what do you think? He danced only four times, though there were several young ladies without partners.'

'But those young ladies were all strangers to me,' Darcy replied. 'And I find it difficult to talk to strangers.'

'Colonel Fitzwilliam,' Elizabeth said, 'Can you tell me why a man like Mr Darcy finds it so difficult to begin a conversation?'

'I can easily answer that question,' Fitzwilliam said. 'It is because he doesn't want to.'

'Some people can talk to strangers about anything, but I cannot,' Darcy replied.

Elizabeth was quick to answer him.

'Other women can play the piano better than I can,' she told Darcy. 'But that is my own fault. I do not practise often enough. If I did practise, I would be able to play as well as other women.'

Darcy smiled at her. 'I understand you,' he said. 'Neither of us is interested in practising so that strangers will think well of us.'

The following morning, Elizabeth was writing a letter to Jane when Mr Darcy arrived. He was surprised to see that Elizabeth was alone. He sat down opposite her, but he did not speak. Elizabeth decided that she must say something.

'You all left Netherfield suddenly last November, Mr Darcy,' Elizabeth said. 'I hope Mr Bingley and his sisters were well when you left London.'

'Yes – thank you.'

After a moment, Elizabeth spoke again.

'I have heard that Mr Bingley does not plan to return to Netherfield for some time,' she said.

'Yes, that is possible,' Darcy replied. 'I don't believe Mr Bingley will ever return to Netherfield.'

Then Darcy went on, 'Mrs Collins must be pleased that she lives so close to her family and friends.'

'So near? Hunsford is fifty miles from Longbourn! It is a long way from home.'

Mr Darcy smiled at her. As he spoke, he moved his chair a little nearer to hers.

'I am sure that you have often been away from Longbourn,' Darcy said.

Then he turned away and looked at a newspaper on the table.

They sat in silence once more. When Charlotte and her sister came back from their walk, Mr Darcy left.

'My dear Lizzy, Mr Darcy must be in love with you!' Charlotte cried. 'What other reason has he for coming here?'

'I expect he is bored at Rosings!' Elizabeth replied.

In the days that followed, Elizabeth often met Mr Darcy when she went out for a walk. He would say a few words and then walk on. One day, Elizabeth met Colonel Fitzwilliam.

'Are you and Mr Darcy leaving Kent on Saturday?' Elizabeth asked him.

'Yes – if Darcy does not change his mind. I shall do what Darcy wants to do.'

'Most people like to please Mr Darcy,' Elizabeth replied. 'Does his sister do everything he wants?'

'Yes, but I look after Miss Darcy too,' Fitzwilliam replied. 'We are both her guardians[53].'

'Are you? And does Miss Darcy give you much trouble?'

Colonel Fitzwilliam looked at Elizabeth anxiously.

'Don't worry. I have heard no gossip about Miss Darcy,'

Elizabeth said quickly. 'I know the Bingleys like her very much. I think you may know them.'

'I know them a little,' Colonel Fitzwilliam answered. 'Mr Bingley is a good friend of Darcy's. I know that Darcy helped Mr Bingley recently. At least, I think Bingley was the man.'

'What do you mean?'

'Darcy told me that he had advised a friend not to get married.'

'Oh, and why did Mr Darcy do that?'

'He told me that it would not have been a sensible marriage.'

Elizabeth walked on in silence. She soon left Colonel Fitzwilliam and went at once to her room.

So Mr Darcy had stopped Mr Bingley from seeing Jane! It was Darcy's pride that had made Jane so unhappy!

Jane would be a good wife. She was the most good-natured and lovely girl. But Mr Darcy was very proud. He did not want his friend to marry one of Mrs Bennet's daughters. So Darcy had taken away Jane's chance of a happy marriage. Elizabeth's anger soon turned to tears.

In the evening, Elizabeth did not go to Rosings with the Collinses. She did not feel well and she did not want to see Mr Darcy.

Elizabeth decided to spend the evening reading Jane's letters again. As she read them, Elizabeth understood how unhappy Jane was. Elizabeth hoped that the next two weeks would pass quickly. She wanted to see her dear sister again.

8

Mr Darcy Speaks

Mr Darcy was going to leave Rosings in two days' time. Elizabeth was thinking about this when the door opened and Mr Darcy came in. He was alone. He asked Elizabeth if she was well, then he sat down. A minute or two later, he stood up and began walking around the room. Elizabeth looked at him in surprise. Then, quickly and anxiously, Mr Darcy began to speak.

'My feelings are too strong. I can hide them no longer. I must tell you how very much I love you!'

Elizabeth blushed and stared at Darcy. She was too surprised to answer.

As Elizabeth did not speak, Mr Darcy went on talking. He spoke well, but Elizabeth heard very little of what he was saying. But she did hear the words 'pride', 'position in society', 'family difficulties'.

Mr Darcy had decided to marry her, although he did not think it would be a sensible marriage! He was sure she would accept his proposal!

At last, Darcy was silent. He waited for Elizabeth's answer.

'It is usual, I know, for a lady to thank a man for his proposal of marriage,' Elizabeth said in an angry voice. 'But I dislike you so much that I cannot thank you. I have never expected you to think well of me. I now understand how much you despise[54] my family. I understand that you love me, although you do not want to. You cannot be surprised that I refuse your proposal.'

Mr Darcy went pale with anger. He waited for a few minutes. Then he replied, 'So this is your answer. You have not refused me very politely. But that is of little importance.'

Elizabeth answered angrily.

'Your proposal was not polite,' she said. 'And I could never marry the man who has made my dear sister so unhappy!'

Darcy looked very surprised, but said nothing.

'Mr Darcy, you took your friend away from my sister. You made them both unhappy.' Elizabeth said quietly.

'I did take Bingley away from your sister,' Darcy replied coldly.

'I have another reason for disliking you,' Elizabeth went on. 'Mr Wickham has told me what you did to him. Because of you, Mr Wickham lost the living he was promised by your father. Because of

Mr Darcy Speaks

you, he is poor.'

Darcy walked across the room with quick, angry steps.

'So this is your opinion of me!' he cried. 'Thank you for telling me my faults.

'I could have hidden my feelings, but I did not,' Darcy went on. 'Should I be pleased that your family has a lower position in society than mine?'

Elizabeth was almost too angry to speak.

'You despise my family,' she said, 'and I despise you. Your words are not those of a gentleman.'

Mr Darcy could not reply. Elizabeth went on speaking, more calmly now.

'I could never have accepted your proposal,' she said. 'From the first moment I saw you, Mr Darcy, I disliked your vanity and pride. You do not care for the feelings of others. You are the last man in the world I could ever think of marrying!'

'You have said enough, madam,' Mr Darcy answered. 'I understand you very well. I am sorry for what has happened. I wish you happiness for the future.'

Mr Darcy bowed and left the room. Elizabeth heard the front door shut behind him.

Elizabeth was angry and confused. She sat down and started to cry. She could not believe what had happened to her. Mr Darcy had proposed! He had been in love with her for many months!

But, because of Darcy's pride, Jane was unhappy and Wickham was poor. Pride like Darcy's was wrong. Crying bitterly, Elizabeth ran to her room.

———

When Elizabeth woke up the following morning, she was still very unhappy. After breakfast, she went for a walk by herself. She walked up the lane and stopped for a moment to look at the park. Elizabeth was unhappy but she was enjoying the beauty of the spring day.

Then Elizabeth saw Mr Darcy. She knew that he had seen her. Elizabeth was beginning to walk away, when she saw that Mr Darcy was holding out a letter.

'I hoped to meet you,' he said quietly. 'Would you please read this letter?' He bowed, handed her the letter and walked away.

Elizabeth opened the letter at once. It was very long. She walked slowly down the lane and began to read.

... Do not be afraid, madam, that I am repeating the proposal that I made last night. You have told me your feelings. Our conversation should now be forgotten. However, yesterday evening you made two accusations[55] against me. I now wish to explain my behaviour – first of all towards your sister and Mr Bingley.

It was soon clear to me, as to everyone else, that Bingley admired your sister. But I had seen him in love before. I did not become anxious until I heard that a marriage between them was expected. I then watched

Bingley closely. His feelings for your sister were very strong. But, as far as I could see, your sister was not in love with Bingley. I was glad, because I had noticed the foolish behaviour of your younger sisters. Forgive me if I hurt you. You and your sister Jane, have always behaved correctly.

When I discovered that Bingley's sisters were also worried about their brother, we all followed Bingley to London. I told him why I thought the marriage was wrong. I also told him that, in my opinion, Miss Bennet did not love him. Bingley believed me. I must tell you that, later, I did not tell Bingley that your sister was in London. I am sorry if I hurt Jane, but I still think that I did the right thing.

Your second accusation was about my behaviour towards Mr Wickham. This is a much more serious accusation because I have known him since I was a child. Also, my father cared for him very much. Let me explain what happened.

For many years, George Wickham's father was steward of the Pemberley estate. My father was happy to help Mr Wickham's son and he paid for his education. My father wanted George Wickham to become a clergyman. I was the same age as Wickham and I soon found out the truth about him. He could hide his weak character and bad behaviour from my father, but not from me.

My father died five years ago. He had arranged for Wickham to have the living at Pemberley. Wickham also inherited £1000 from my father. Six months after my father died, Wickham told me that he wished to study law. But Wickham had no money. I sent him £3000. Wickham was now living in London and I did not hear from him again for three years. Then, to my surprise, he said he was going to be a clergyman and asked for the living at Pemberley. I refused to give him the living and did not see him again until last summer.

I now have to tell you something about my sister. I know you will keep it a secret. My sister, Georgiana, is ten years younger than me. Colonel Fitzwilliam and I are her guardians. About a year ago, Georgiana left school. She went to live in our London house with her friend, Mrs Younge. Unfortunately, Mr Wickham knew Mrs Younge well. When Mrs Younge went on holiday with Georgiana, Wickham followed them. My dear sister was only fifteen and she thought she was in love with Wickham. She agreed to elope[56] with him. Wickham, of course, wanted my sister's money. He also wanted to take revenge[57] on me. Thank God, Georgiana told me everything. Mrs Younge was sent away and Wickham left at once.

That, madam, is the truth about Mr Wickham. I hope you now understand my feelings towards him. I do not blame you for disliking me. You did not know the truth. Colonel Fitzwilliam knows that all this is true. Speak to him if you do not believe me. I shall try to give you this letter before we leave Rosings.

God bless you.
Fitzwilliam Darcy

Elizabeth read the letter quickly. At first, she was angry. Then she was horrified. Elizabeth remembered her first conversation with Wickham. Wickham had said that he had no fear of Mr Darcy. But Wickham had stayed away from the Netherfield Ball. And Wickham was now interested in Miss King who had inherited a fortune.

'How foolishly I have behaved!' Elizabeth said to herself. 'And I thought I was so clever at studying people. I thought I understood people's characters! But my vanity has made me foolish. How little I know of other people's characters – or my own!'

Elizabeth read the first part of the letter again. What Darcy said was true. Jane did not show her feelings. When Elizabeth read what Darcy said about her and Jane, she felt a little better. But she blushed with embarrassment when she read again what he said about the rest of her family. It was true. They had all behaved badly.

Elizabeth walked around the park for two hours. When she returned to the house, she was told that Colonel Fitzwilliam and Darcy had called to say goodbye. They were leaving early the next morning. Elizabeth was not sorry that she had refused Mr Darcy's proposal. She had no wish to see him again. She did not like him, but she respected him now.

At last it was time for Elizabeth and Maria Lucas to leave Hunsford. They said goodbye to Lady Catherine. The first part of their journey was to London. They were going to stay with the Gardiners for a few days. Then they were going home with Jane to Longbourn.

9

The Militia Goes to Brighton

Elizabeth, Jane and Maria Lucas left London in the second week of May. Kitty and Lydia met them in a large town near Longbourn. Mr Bennet had allowed the girls to take the carriage.

'Are you surprised to see us?' Lydia cried. 'Look I bought this hat while we were waiting. It isn't very pretty, is it? But I don't care what I wear this summer. The militia are leaving Meryton in two weeks' time!'

'Are they?' said Elizabeth. She was very pleased.

'Yes, they are going to Brighton. I want Father to take us to Brighton for the summer. I have news for you too, Lizzy. It is about dear Wickham. He is not going to marry Miss King after all!'

When they were all in the carriage, Lydia went on chattering happily.

'Well, what has happened to you both since you went away?' Lydia asked. 'Have you met any pleasant men? I hoped one of you would have found a husband! Jane is almost twenty-three. I would hate to be twenty-three and unmarried! I would like to marry before any of you.'

Lydia went on chattering and gossiping. The journey passed and they were soon at Longbourn. Mrs Bennet thought Jane looked as beautiful as ever and Mr Bennet was very pleased to have Elizabeth at home again. In the afternoon, Lydia wanted them all to walk into Meryton, but Elizabeth refused. She did not want to see

Wickham. And she did not want people to say that the Bennet girls were always chattering to the officers.

When Elizabeth was alone with Jane, she told her about Mr Darcy's proposal. Jane was very surprised, but she tried to think of something kind to say.

'It was wrong of Mr Darcy to think that you would accept his proposal. But your refusal must have disappointed him,' Jane said.

'Do you blame me for refusing him?'

'Blame you? Oh, no! And you were right to tell Mr Darcy what you knew about him and Wickham,' Jane said.

'You may change your mind when I tell you what happened the next day!' her sister replied.

Elizabeth then told Jane what Mr Darcy had written about Wickham. How unhappy Jane was to hear of it! She was pleased that Mr Darcy was a good man, but Wickham could not be so bad!

'No, Jane,' Elizabeth said, smiling. 'They cannot both be right. You must decide. I think Mr Darcy is a good man. Mr Wickham is certainly not. But he made us think he was good.'

'I have always had a good opinion of Mr Darcy, Lizzy,' Jane replied.

'And I thought I was clever when I disliked him immediately!' Elizabeth said, smiling. 'It is so easy to say clever things about someone you dislike!'

'You are laughing now, Lizzy,' Jane said kindly, 'but I am sure you did not laugh when you first read Darcy's letter.'

'I did not – I wanted you with me. I was so unhappy that I cried. I was ashamed[58] of my own prejudice too. But I want your help. Should our friends know the truth about Wickham?'

'I don't believe that is necessary,' Jane said quietly. 'What is your opinion, Lizzy?'

'I agree with you. The people of Meryton are very prejudiced against Mr Darcy. They would never change their minds. Wickham will be leaving soon. There is no need to tell everyone what kind of man he is.'

'You are right,' Jane replied.

The Militia Goes To Brighton

Elizabeth did not tell Jane what Mr Darcy had said about her and Mr Bingley. She did not tell Jane that Bingley loved her. She did not want to be unkind. Elizabeth knew that her sister still loved Bingley.

'Well, Lizzy,' Mrs Bennet said one day, 'I do not think Bingley is coming back to Netherfield. And Jane did not see him when she was in London. Well, he must do as he likes. But he will be sorry when Jane dies of a broken heart[59]!'

———

The militia was leaving Meryton. All the young ladies in Meryton except Jane and Elizabeth were upset.

'What are we to do?' Lydia cried. 'How can you smile, Lizzy? I am sure that my heart will break! I want to go to Brighton too! But Father will not allow me to go.'

Soon Lydia was happy again. Mrs Forster, the young wife of Colonel Forster, invited Lydia to stay with her in Brighton. Kitty cried and cried.

'Why couldn't Mrs Forster ask me too?' Kitty asked. 'I am two years older than Lydia!'

Mrs Bennet was delighted. But Elizabeth was very worried. She went to her father and asked him to make Lydia stay at home. But Mr Bennet said Lydia could go to Brighton.

'Lydia will not be happy until she has done something foolish,' Mr Bennet said. 'She can be foolish in Brighton. I don't want her to be foolish here.'

'But people are already talking about Lydia's behaviour,' Elizabeth replied. 'She is only sixteen and, if you do not stop her, Father, she will always behave badly.

'She will always be silly and thoughtless. And Kitty will always behave like Lydia too. And we shall be blamed for their foolish behaviour!'

Mr Bennet saw that Elizabeth was serious. He smiled and took hold of her hand.

'Do not worry, my love,' he said. 'You and Jane will always be respected – although you have three very silly sisters. Let Lydia go to Brighton. Colonel Forster is a sensible man and he will look after her.'

The last day before the militia left Meryton, Mr Wickham and several other officers had dinner at Longbourn House. Wickham asked Elizabeth about her holiday at Hunsford. She told him that Colonel Fitzwilliam and Mr Darcy had been at Rosings.

'How long did they stay?' Wickham asked.

'Three weeks.'

'And you saw them often?'

'Yes, almost every day,' Elizabeth replied.

'Colonel Fitzwilliam's manners are very different from his cousin's,' Wickham said quietly.

'Yes, very different,' Elizabeth replied. 'but I know Mr Darcy better now and I like him better.'

'I am surprised,' Wickham said. 'Are his manners better? I cannot believe that his character has changed.'

'Oh, no,' Elizabeth replied. 'Mr Darcy's character is the same as it always was. But I understand him better now.'

Mr Wickham looked worried for a moment. Then he spoke again.

'You know my feelings about Mr Darcy,' Wickham said. 'I am sure he wants to please his aunt. He is afraid of her, I know. And, of course, he wishes to please Miss de Bourgh because he plans to marry her.'

Elizabeth smiled, but she did not continue the conversation. At the end of the evening, they said goodbye to each other politely.

Lydia returned with Mrs Forster to Meryton. They were leaving for Brighton early the following morning. Kitty cried – but her tears were tears of anger. Mrs Bennet told Lydia to enjoy herself as much as she could.

―――

Elizabeth was glad that Wickham had left Meryton. Now she began to look forward to her holiday in the Lake District with her uncle and aunt.

When the holiday was only two weeks away, a letter arrived from Mrs Gardiner. The Gardiners' plans had changed. Mr Gardiner could not leave London until the middle of July and he could only be away for three weeks. The Lake District was too far away so they were going to Derbyshire.

Elizabeth was disappointed. And she remembered that Pemberley, Mr Darcy's home, was in Derbyshire.

10
Elizabeth in Derbyshire

The journey with the Gardiners was pleasant. They were cheerful and intelligent. Elizabeth enjoyed travelling with them and she was delighted with everything she saw.

They passed through Oxfordshire and the Midlands, and at last they arrived in the little town of Lambton, in Derbyshire. They were going to stay at an inn in the town. Mrs Gardiner had lived in Lambton before she was married.

. 'Pemberley is only a mile or two away from Lambton,' Mrs Gardiner said. 'Would you like to see the place you've heard so much about? Wickham lived there when he was young.'

But Elizabeth did not think that she should go to Pemberley.

'Dear Aunt, we have seen so many beautiful houses[60],' she said. 'Do you want to see another one?'

'But Pemberley is not only a very beautiful house,' Mrs Gardiner replied. 'The gardens are delightful too and the woods are very lovely.'

Elizabeth was very worried that she might meet Mr Darcy. But someone at the inn where they were staying told her that the Darcys were away. So Elizabeth agreed to visit Pemberley.

There was a very large park around the house. As they drove through the park, Elizabeth looked at the woods on either side of the road. At last, she saw Pemberley. The house was a large, very handsome building, with beautiful gardens. Around the park there were hills covered with trees. A stream ran through a valley below the house. Elizabeth thought it was the most beautiful place she had ever seen.

They drove down a hill, crossed a bridge and drove up to the doors of Pemberley. Elizabeth felt worried again. Perhaps Mr Darcy was there after all!

They rang the doorbell. The housekeeper[61] told them she would

Elizabeth in Derbyshire

be delighted to show them the house. They followed her through the entrance hall into the dining-room. It was a large, handsome room, with fine furniture and carpets. Elizabeth looked around her. How beautiful everything was!

As they walked through the house, Elizabeth saw that every room was very handsome.

This would have been my home if I had accepted Darcy's proposal, Elizabeth thought.

'We believe that the master of the house is away at present,' Mr Gardiner was saying to the housekeeper. Her name was Mrs Reynolds.

'Yes,' Mrs Reynolds replied. 'But Mr Darcy is coming here tomorrow, with several of his friends.'

Mrs Gardiner was looking at some paintings.

'Look, Elizabeth,' she said. 'Do you like this portrait of Mr Wickham?'

Elizabeth could not answer.

'That is a picture of the son of old Mr Darcy's steward,' Mrs Reynolds said. 'Old Mr Darcy liked him very much. Mr Wickham is in the militia now. I'm afraid he is not a very pleasant young man.'

'But this,' the housekeeper went on, 'is my master.' And she pointed proudly to a small portrait of Mr Darcy.

'It is a handsome face,' Mrs Gardiner said. 'Does the picture look like him, Lizzy?'

Mrs Reynolds turned and looked at Elizabeth.

'Do you know Mr Darcy?' she asked. 'Don't you agree that he is a handsome gentleman?'

'Yes, very handsome,' Elizabeth replied, blushing.

'In a room upstairs, you can see a larger portrait of Mr Darcy,' Mrs Reynolds told them. 'Look, here is a portrait of Miss Georgiana Darcy. Such a beautiful young lady! She will be here tomorrow, with her brother.'

'Does Mr Darcy often stay at Pemberley?' Mr Gardiner asked.

'No, sir. But Miss Darcy is always here for the summer.'

Elizabeth in Derbyshire

'If your master got married and lived here at Pemberley,' Mr Gardiner said, 'you would see him more often.'

'Yes, sir, but I don't know when he will get married,' the housekeeper answered. 'I do not know anyone who is good enough for Mr Darcy. He is a good-natured and delightful young man.'

Elizabeth was very surprised by these words. She wanted to hear more.

'It must be good to have such a master,' Mr Gardiner said.

'Yes, sir,' said the housekeeper. 'I could not have a better master. He was good-natured as a child and he is the same now.'

Elizabeth could not believe what the housekeeper was saying. Is she really talking about Mr Darcy? she thought.

The housekeeper took them upstairs. 'He is the best master I could have,' she went on. 'And he is a good brother too. Look at this room. Mr Darcy is always thinking of how to please his sister. He has chosen the finest carpets and furniture for her room. Some people call him proud, but I do not agree. He talks less than other young men, I suppose.'

'It is strange that she is talking about Mr Darcy in this way,' Mrs Gardiner whispered to Elizabeth. 'Remember how badly he behaved to our poor friend, Wickham!'

'Perhaps we did not hear the true story,' Elizabeth replied.

They were now standing in a long room, looking at portraits of the Darcy family. Elizabeth walked on until she was standing in front of the picture of Mr Darcy. He was smiling. Elizabeth remembered that he had sometimes smiled at her like this. As Elizabeth stood there, she remembered all that the housekeeper had said about him. Elizabeth began to think more kindly of Mr Darcy.

Some time later, they left the house and went into the gardens. Mr and Mrs Gardiner stopped and turned to look at the house again. Elizabeth walked on and suddenly saw Mr Darcy walking towards her! They both blushed and stopped walking. They stared at each other in surprise. Then Darcy spoke to Elizabeth very politely and Elizabeth replied, although she was very embarrassed. Darcy was as embarrassed as Elizabeth.

Elizabeth remembered that he had sometimes smiled at her like this.

Elizabeth in Derbyshire

They went on talking for a few minutes and then Mr Darcy bowed and walked away.

Mr and Mrs Gardiner now came up to Elizabeth and she walked on with them. Oh, why had she come? Why had Mr Darcy come back a day early? What did he think of her? He must have been very surprised to find her at Pemberley. But how politely he had spoken to her! Elizabeth did not know what to think.

They were now walking along a beautiful path, beside the stream. The park was very beautiful, but Elizabeth could only think of Mr Darcy. She wanted to know what he was thinking. Was he still in love with her or not?

Mrs Gardiner was tired now, so they decided to return to their carriage. Then suddenly Elizabeth saw Mr Darcy coming towards them! She was very surprised. Darcy walked on calmly. He was going to speak to them!

As they met, Elizabeth blushed and smiled.

'Will you introduce me to your friends?' Mr Darcy asked Elizabeth politely.

Elizabeth introduced her uncle and aunt to Mr Darcy. Then Mr Gardiner and Mr Darcy began to talk. Mrs Gardiner looked at her niece. Elizabeth said nothing.

Why is he so different? Elizabeth thought. Is it possible that he still loves me?

After a time, Mrs Gardiner began to walk with her husband. So Elizabeth spoke to Mr Darcy.

'We did not know that you were at Pemberley,' Elizabeth told him quickly. 'Your housekeeper told us that you were not coming until tomorrow.'

'I had some business here,' Mr Darcy answered. 'Mr Bingley and his sisters are coming tomorrow.'

Elizabeth did not answer. She remembered the last time they had spoken of Mr Bingley.

At last, Mr Darcy spoke again.

'My sister very much wants to meet you. May I introduce her to you?'

Elizabeth in Derbyshire

'Why yes ... of course,' Elizabeth replied. 'I would be delighted.'

As Elizabeth and the Gardiners left Pemberley, Elizabeth turned to watch Mr Darcy. He was walking slowly back to the house.

'Mr Darcy is a very polite, quiet young man,' Mr Gardiner said.

'He is not proud and he has fine manners,' Mrs Gardiner said. 'Why did you tell us that Mr Darcy was so unpleasant, Lizzy? I am surprised that he behaved so badly to Mr Wickham. He has a kind and intelligent face!'

Elizabeth now had to explain that she had learnt more about Wickham while she was at Hunsford. She told Mrs Gardiner that Wickham had behaved badly towards Mr Darcy. But she did not tell her aunt about Wickham's elopement with Georgiana Darcy.

Mrs Gardiner was surprised, but there were other things to interest them and they did not talk any more about Wickham.

―――

The following morning, the Darcys' carriage stopped outside the inn where Elizabeth and the Gardiners were staying. Elizabeth saw their carriage from the window of the inn. She blushed and looked very anxious. The Gardiners were surprised at her embarrassment.

Miss Darcy and her brother came in. Then Mr Darcy introduced his sister to Elizabeth and the Gardiners. Miss Darcy was tall. She had a pretty face and her manners were very good.

Georgiana Darcy was not proud but very shy[62] and polite. Elizabeth was delighted.

Darcy told Elizabeth that Bingley was also hoping to see her. In a few minutes, Bingley arrived. He spoke to Elizabeth politely and kindly and asked about her family.

Bingley said to Elizabeth, 'We last met on the 26th of November – more than eight months ago.'

As the young people talked to each other, Mr and Mrs Gardiner watched with great interest. They could see that Mr Darcy admired Elizabeth. And they decided that he was in love with her. They were not sure that Elizabeth was in love with him.

Bingley told Elizabeth that he had many questions to ask about his friends in Hertfordshire. He wanted to talk to Elizabeth about Jane!

Before they left the inn, Mr Darcy invited Mr and Mrs Gardiner and Elizabeth to dinner at Pemberley.

That night, Elizabeth lay awake for two hours. How did she feel about Mr Darcy? She did not hate him. She now believed he was a kind and intelligent man. It was clear that Mr Darcy wanted to please her. And he wanted her uncle and aunt to think well of him. He must still love her!

―――

Mrs Gardiner and Elizabeth had said they would call on Miss Darcy the following morning.

When they reached the house, Elizabeth and her aunt were taken to a beautiful room.

Miss Darcy spoke to them shyly. Miss Bingley and her sister smiled coldly. Then the gentlemen came in. Elizabeth saw that everyone was watching her and Darcy. Miss Bingley could not hide her anger.

'I believe the militia has left Meryton, Miss Elizabeth!' Miss Bingley said loudly. 'That must be a great disappointment to your sisters!'

Elizabeth saw that Mr Darcy was angry and that his sister was upset. When it was time for the visitors to leave, Darcy walked with them to their carriage.

As soon as Elizabeth left the room, Caroline Bingley began to talk about her. Miss Bingley was still talking when Mr Darcy returned.

'Miss Bennet is not so attractive now, Mr Darcy!' Miss Bingley cried. 'Her skin is so brown and rough from the sun.'

'The sun does make people's faces brown if they travel in the summer,' Mr Darcy answered quietly.

But Miss Bingley had not finished talking about Elizabeth. 'I do not think her face is attractive. And I don't think her eyes are beautiful although some people have admired them. In Hertfordshire, it was often said that Miss Bennet was beautiful!

'But I remember your words, Mr Darcy,' Miss Bingley went on. 'You said: "If Miss Bennet is beautiful, then her mother is clever!" '

Darcy spoke at last.

'I said that when I first met her,' he replied. 'but for many months now, I have thought Miss Elizabeth Bennet one of the most beautiful women I know.'

Darcy then left the room. Miss Bingley's words had hurt no one but herself.

That evening, Mrs Gardiner and Elizabeth talked about everything and everyone they had seen at Pemberley. The only person they did not talk about was Mr Darcy. But Elizabeth very much wanted to know what Mrs Gardiner thought of him. And Mrs Gardiner very much wanted to know what her niece thought of that gentleman!

11

Bad News

Elizabeth was waiting for a letter from Jane. Then, three days after they had arrived at Lambton, two letters from Jane arrived. In the first one, Jane wrote:

Dearest Lizzy,

Something serious has happened. We are all well, but I have something terrible to tell you about Lydia. We heard last night that she has run away with one of the officers – with Wickham. We are very surprised and upset, although Kitty tells us that she knew of Lydia's plan.

They have eloped. It was a very foolish and thoughtless thing to do. What will happen if Wickham will not marry Lydia? ...

Bad News

Elizabeth quickly opened the other letter.

Dearest Lizzy,

I have more bad news for you – worse than before. Lydia and Wickham have not got married. Colonel Forster knows Wickham and Lydia have gone to London. My poor mother is too ill to leave her room and father is very angry with Kitty. Dearest Lizzy, please come home soon. We all miss you ...

And then Jane had written this note at the bottom of the letter:

... Please come home as soon as possible. My father is going to London to find Lydia and Wickham. But he would like our uncle Gardiner to meet him in London. Father wants our uncle to help him to find ...

'Oh, I must find my uncle!' Elizabeth cried as she ran towards the door. At that very moment, the door opened and Mr Darcy came in.

'I must find my uncle,' Elizabeth cried. 'Something terrible has happened.'

'My God, what is the matter?' Mr Darcy said. 'I will send someone to look for him. You cannot go yourself – you are not well.'

Elizabeth sat down. She looked very pale and ill. Darcy sent a servant from the inn to find the Gardiners.

Then he came back into the room.

'Can I get you a glass of wine?' Darcy asked gently. 'You are very ill ...'

'I am not ill,' Elizabeth replied quietly. 'But I have been upset by some terrible news from Longbourn.' She started to cry as she spoke.

'I must tell you, Mr Darcy,' Elizabeth said. 'My youngest sister has eloped with Mr Wickham. You know that Wickham will not marry Lydia!'

Darcy stared at Elizabeth.

'I knew Wickham's character was bad!' Elizabeth went on. 'But I did not tell my family and it is too late now!'

Bad News

'I am shocked and horrified,' Darcy said. 'But are you sure they have run away together?'

'Oh, yes. Lydia and Wickham left Brighton on Sunday night. We know that they are in London.

'My father has gone there,' Elizabeth went on, 'and Jane has asked for my uncle's help. But what can he do?'

Darcy did not answer. He walked up and down the room. His face was hard and serious.

How could Mr Darcy love her now? Elizabeth thought. Lydia's elopement was a great disgrace[63] for the Bennet family. And it was then, at last, that Elizabeth knew she loved Darcy. Tears fell from Elizabeth's eyes and she covered her face with her handkerchief.

Then Darcy spoke very kindly. 'I wish I could say something to make you feel better – but I know it is impossible at the moment. I am sorry that you will not be able to visit my sister at Pemberley today.'

'Oh, I had forgotten! Please tell Miss Darcy that we have had to go home. Please promise me that you will hide the truth as long as possible.'

Mr Darcy promised and, with one last look at Elizabeth, he left the room.

I shall never see him again, Elizabeth thought. How strange our friendship has been! I wish it did not have to end!

Then she thought of Lydia once more. Wickham would never marry her. Lydia was a foolish, thoughtless girl with no money.

At this moment, Mr and Mrs Gardiner came in and Elizabeth told them the terrible news. They agreed to leave Derbyshire as soon as possible.

'But what about our visit to Pemberley?' Mrs Gardiner asked. 'What can we tell Mr Darcy?'

'I have told Mr Darcy myself,' Elizabeth replied. 'He was here this morning. He understands everything.'

Understands everything? Mrs Gardiner thought. Are Elizabeth and Darcy's feelings for each other so strong? I wish I knew!

But there was no time for any questions. There were many things

Bad News

to do. In an hour they were ready and, very soon, they were on their way back to Longbourn.

'Wickham must be planning to marry Lydia,' Mr Gardiner said. 'She has family and friends who will expect them to marry. Wickham must be afraid of disgrace for himself and for Lydia.'

'But Jane and I know Wickham's character,' Elizabeth answered sadly. 'He is a dishonest, and deceitful[64] man.'

'Are you sure?' Mrs Gardiner asked.

'Yes, I am,' Elizabeth replied, blushing. 'He has told many lies. He has never told the truth about himself and the Darcy family.

'When I was at Hunsford,' Elizabeth went on. 'I learnt a lot about Wickham. I cannot tell you everything. But when I returned home, the militia was about to leave Meryton so I decided to say nothing. I did not know that Wickham was interested in Lydia.'

They reached Longbourn in about twenty-four hours. Elizabeth ran into the house and went to find Jane.

'We have had no news yet,' Jane said, 'but I feel much happier now that our uncle is here.'

'Is our father in London?' Elizabeth asked her sister anxiously.

'Yes, he went on Tuesday. Our mother is upstairs. She will be so pleased to see you all.'

They all went to Mrs Bennet's room. She was crying. 'If I had been able to go to Brighton, this would never have happened!' Mrs Bennet cried. 'My poor dear Lydia! Mrs Forster should have taken more care of her!

'And now Mr Bennet is in London. When he meets Wickham, he is sure to fight him. Mr Bennet will be killed and Mr Collins will make us leave this house!'

'That will never happen,' Mr Gardiner said. 'I am going to London at once, to find Mr Bennet,' he went on. 'Then we can plan what to do.'

'Oh, my dear brother, when you are in London, find Lydia and Wickham and make them marry!' Mrs Bennet cried. 'Make them marry at once! And stop Mr Bennet from fighting Wickham. Tell him I am ill. I am sure you will arrange everything!'

At dinner, the four sisters talked about what had happened. Kitty had been crying, but Mary, as usual, was calm.

'I am sorry this has happened,' Mary said to Elizabeth, 'but we must look after each other and not listen to unkind gossip.

'There is a lesson to be learnt from Lydia's behaviour,' Mary went on. 'It is this. When a young woman turns away with a man, she is disgraced. This is what I have read. Once a woman has been disgraced, people will always think she is bad.'

Elizabeth was too unhappy to reply. Mary is as silly as Lydia, she thought.

The following day, Mr and Mrs Gardiner went to London. When Mr Gardiner wrote, two days later, he had no good news. Wickham had left many debts in Brighton and owed about £1000. Mr Gardiner said that Mr Bennet was returning to Longbourn the following day.

The next day Mr Bennet arrived home. He was very unhappy.

'I have been a bad father,' Mr Bennet said to Elizabeth. 'Why didn't I listen to you, Lizzy? Why didn't I make Lydia stay at home?'

12

Mr and Mrs George Wickham

Two days later, a letter arrived for Mr Bennet and he took it into the library at once. He called Jane and Elizabeth to see him.

'Oh, Father, what is the news – good or bad?' Elizabeth asked anxiously.

'There cannot be any good news,' Mr Bennet answered. 'You read the letter, Lizzy. Tell me what your uncle says.'

Elizabeth took the letter and read it quickly.

'My uncle has found Wickham and Lydia,' she said. 'They are not married but he hopes they soon will be.'

Elizabeth turned over the page. 'Mr Wickham has agreed to a

settlement[65] and he will have a little money left, after his debts are paid. Mr Gardiner writes that he will arrange everything, if you agree, sir,' Elizabeth said to her father. 'And Lydia will stay with the Gardiners until she is married.'

'That *is* good news, sir,' Jane said. 'Wickham cannot be as bad as we thought!'

'There are two things I want to know,' Mr Bennet said. 'How much money has your uncle paid Wickham? And how can I ever pay the money back to your uncle?'

'What do you mean, sir?' Jane asked.

'I mean that no man would marry Lydia for a small settlement. Wickham's a fool if he takes less than £10 000! And how is the money to be repaid? But I must agree. I shall answer your uncle's letter at once.'

'May we take his letter to our mother?' Jane asked.

'Do what you like. But leave me alone now, please.'

When Mrs Bennet heard the news, she was very excited.

'What delightful news!' Mrs Bennet cried. 'My dear Lydia will be married – married at sixteen! I want to see her soon - and dear Wickham too! But she must have new clothes - I must ask your father how much money he will give her. Mrs Wickham! How fine it sounds – and she was only sixteen last June!'

Mrs Bennet decided that she was well now, and she went downstairs. All her unhappiness was forgotten. Her plan was to find a house near to Longbourn House where Lydia and Wickham could live. Mr Bennet allowed his wife to chatter for a few minutes and then he spoke to her severely.

'Mrs Bennet, listen to me! There is one house in this neighbourhood where your daughter and her husband will never come – Longbourn House. They can never come here.'

And then Mr Bennet said that he was not going to buy Lydia any wedding clothes. Mrs Bennet was horrified.

Mr Gardiner's next letter brought important news. Mr Wickham was going to leave the militia and join the regular army[66], as soon as his debts had been paid. After the wedding, Wickham and Lydia were going to join his regiment which was stationed in the north of England. Mr Gardiner said that Lydia wanted to see her family before leaving. Jane and Elizabeth asked their father to allow Lydia to come and see them. At last he agreed.

Lydia's wedding-day arrived. Lydia and Wickham were married in London and travelled to Longbourn for dinner. All the Bennets were waiting for them. They heard the carriage and then Lydia's voice. In a minute, the door was opened and Lydia ran into the room. She was noisy and cheerful. Wickham was smiling and pleasant. Neither Lydia nor Wickham said they were sorry for all the trouble they had brought to the Bennets.

'It is only three months since I went away!' Lydia cried, 'and here I am again – married. Don't you think my husband is a delightful man, Mother?'

A day or two later, Lydia was sitting with her two eldest sisters.

'Lizzy, I haven't told you about my wedding,' Lydia began. 'I am sure you and Jane want to know everything. I was married on Monday, you know, at eleven o'clock. I went to the church with my aunt and uncle – and my dear Wickham and Mr Darcy met us there.'

'Mr Darcy!' Elizabeth cried.

'Oh dear,' Lydia said quickly. 'I promised Wickham I would not tell you that Mr Darcy was there!'

'Then we must not say any more about it,' Jane said.

Elizabeth had to agree with Jane. But she wanted to know why Mr Darcy had been at her sister's wedding. There was only one way to find out. Elizabeth wrote at once to Mrs Gardiner.

An answer came very quickly. Elizabeth went to a quiet place in the garden and began to read her aunt's letter.

My dear niece,

I have much to tell you. Your uncle and I thought you knew all about Mr Darcy and his help with Lydia and Wickham's marriage.

Neither Lydia nor Wickham said they were sorry for all the trouble they had brought to the Bennets.

> *Darcy left Derbyshire the day after we did. He knew where Wickham usually stayed in London and he found Lydia and Wickham there. Darcy saw Wickham alone several times. At last he made Wickham agree to marry Lydia. Darcy said he would pay all Wickham's debts and give him a large amount of money. Darcy then asked your uncle to agree to the plan. We thought you knew everything. You must tell no one – except perhaps Jane. Lydia stayed at our house until the wedding. As you know, Mr Darcy came to the church with Wickham. Mr Darcy had dinner with us, the day after the wedding. I must tell you Lizzy, how much I like him. He is an intelligent man with a very fine character. My dear Lizzy, you have a lot to tell me! Do let me visit you at Pemberley!*
>
> *Yours very sincerely,*
> *Mary Gardiner*

Elizabeth did not know what to think. Mr Darcy had helped her family so much. He had forgotten his pride so that he could help Lydia and Wickham. And the Gardiners believed that Darcy had done everything because he loved Elizabeth! And Elizabeth had behaved so badly towards him.

Elizabeth walked in the garden for some time and then she saw Wickham coming towards her.

'My dear Elizabeth,' he said, 'I am so delighted to see you again. Jane has told me that you have been in Derbyshire, and that you saw Pemberley. It is a fine house. Did the housekeeper, Mrs Reynolds, talk about me?'

'Well, yes, she did,' Elizabeth answered.

'And what did she say?'

'She said that you had gone into the militia. And she also said that you had behaved badly. She could have been wrong, of course.'

'Yes, of course. And I believe you also met Darcy and his sister there?'

'Yes, Mr Darcy introduced me to his sister. I liked her very much.'

'I was surprised to see Darcy in town last month,' Wickham said.

'Perhaps he was preparing for his marriage to Miss de Bourgh,'

Elizabeth said.

Then she looked at Wickham and smiled. 'Let us forget the past, Mr Wickham – we are brother and sister now.'

Wickham smiled. Then he bowed and walked quickly away.

It was soon time for Mr and Mrs Wickham to leave for the north of England where Wickham had to join his army regiment.

'Oh, my dear Lydia!' Mrs Bennet cried. 'When shall I see you again?'

'Oh, I don't know – in two or three years perhaps,' Lydia said, laughing. 'My sisters will have to write to me.'

13

Mr Bingley Returns to Netherfield

Some good news soon reached Longbourn House. Mr Bingley was returning to Netherfield Hall and would be staying there for several months.

Mrs Bennet looked at Jane when she heard the news. Jane blushed, but said nothing.

'I know I looked upset, Lizzy,' Jane told her sister later. 'But it was only for a moment. It is not important that Mr Bingley is returning to Netherfield. Mr Bingley will not call here. But I am pleased that his sisters are not coming.'

But Elizabeth had spoken to Bingley in Derbyshire. She knew why he was returning to Netherfield. Mrs Bennet also thought that Bingley was coming back to see Jane.

'As soon as Mr Bingley arrives at Netherfield, my dear,' Mrs Bennet said to her husband, 'you must call on him.'

'No, no. You made me call on him last year,' Mr Bennet replied. 'You promised that if I went to see Mr Bingley, he would marry one of our daughters. He did not. I refuse to go again. He knows where we live. He can come here, if he wants to see us.'

Mr Bingley Returns to Netherfield

'Well then, I shall have a dinner-party and invite Mr Bingley,' Mrs Bennet said.

Mr Bingley arrived at Netherfield at last. And before Mrs Bennet had time to invite him to have dinner, the young man called at Longbourn House. Kitty, who was looking out of the window, saw him first.

'Here is Mr Bingley, Mother,' Kitty cried. 'And there is someone else with him. Who can it be? It looks like that tall, proud man who was here before – Mr What's-his-name!'

Elizabeth did not move, but her mother ran to the window.

'Well, any friend of Bingley's is always welcome,' Mrs Bennet cried. 'But I must say, I do not like Mr Darcy!'

The two gentlemen came in. Jane spoke to them calmly but Elizabeth could not look at Darcy. She blushed and looked away. Darcy looked at Jane as often as he looked at Elizabeth. Elizabeth was disappointed, but at last she was able to ask Mr Darcy about his sister.

Mrs Bennet chattered happily.

'It is a long time since you went away, Mr Bingley,' Mrs Bennet said. 'People said that you would never come back. There have been many changes in the neighbourhood. Miss Lucas is married and so is one of my daughters.'

Mr Bingley congratulated Mrs Bennet.

'Yes, I am delighted that my daughter has married such a fine young man,' Mrs Bennet went on. 'But I am sorry that Lydia has to live so far away. Her husband is now in the army, you know.'

Elizabeth was ashamed of the way her mother chattered and gossiped. Then Mrs Bennet invited the gentlemen to dinner on Tuesday and, in a few minutes, both gentlemen had left.

Why did Mr Darcy come at all? Elizabeth thought. He sat and said nothing. If he cares for me, why doesn't he say something?

'Now that I have met Mr Bingley again, I do not feel worried,' Jane told Elizabeth. 'I am pleased that he is coming for dinner here on Tuesday. Everyone will see that we are not in love with each other.'

'Oh, Jane!' Elizabeth laughed. 'I think Mr Bingley still loves you!'

Mr Darcy and Mr Bingley came the following Tuesday. Jane smiled happily at Mr Bingley and he went to sit next to her. Jane looked very beautiful. Elizabeth could see that Bingley admired her very much.

Elizabeth was not as happy as Jane. At dinner, Mr Darcy sat next to Mrs Bennet at the other end of the table. He and Mrs Bennet spoke very little to each other.

Elizabeth hoped that Darcy would talk to her after dinner.

If he does not speak to me, I shall not think about him again, she thought.

But there was no time for Darcy and Elizabeth to speak to each other. Everyone played cards and Elizabeth and Darcy were not sitting near each other, but Mr Darcy often looked across the room at Elizabeth.

Is he playing cards as badly as I am? she thought.

After a few hours the gentlemen left.

'I think everything went very well,' Mrs Bennet said. 'Everyone liked the food and Jane looked very beautiful. I know Mr Bingley thought so.'

A few days later, Mr Bingley called at Longbourn House again. Mr Darcy had left for London and was going to return in a week. Mr Bingley had dinner with the Bennets again. After dinner, Mrs Bennet made sure that Bingley and Jane sat next to each other all evening.

The next day, Bingley had dinner at Longbourn again. After dinner, Mrs Bennet left Jane and Bingley to talk together.

Later, Jane came and found Elizabeth.

'Oh, Lizzy,' she said. 'I am the happiest girl in the world! Oh, why isn't everyone as happy as me? I must tell my mother! Bingley has asked me to marry him. He has gone to speak to our father. Oh, Lizzy, I never knew I could be so happy!'

Everyone was happy. When Bingley had at last left, Mr Bennet spoke to his eldest daughter. 'Jane, I congratulate you,' he said. 'You are a good girl. You and Bingley will be very happy together.'

'They are sure to be happy. Mr Bingley has a very good income,' Mrs Bennet said.

Now Bingley came to Longbourn House every day.

'He did love me last November, Lizzy!' Jane told her sister. 'He didn't come back, because he thought I didn't love him. And his sisters didn't tell him I was in London last spring.'

Very soon, the whole of Meryton knew that Jane and Bingley were engaged.

Only a few weeks before, when Lydia had eloped, everyone had talked about the Bennets' disgrace. But now everyone was congratulating Jane. She had become engaged to a wealthy gentleman from a good family. The Bennets were the most fortunate family in the world!

14
Lady Catherine Asks Some Questions

One morning, a week later, Mrs Bennet was sitting with Elizabeth and Kitty when they heard the sound of a carriage outside. In a few minutes, the door was opened and their visitor came in. It was Lady Catherine de Bourgh!

Lady Catherine looked around her, bowed to Elizabeth and sat down.

'I hope you are well, Miss Bennet,' Lady Catherine said. 'That lady must be your mother. And that must be one of your sisters.'

'Yes, madam,' Mrs Bennet said. 'This is my daughter, Kitty. My youngest daughter, Lydia, was married five weeks ago. My eldest is out walking with a young man whom she will soon marry. Are Mr and Mrs Collins well?'

'Yes, very well.'

Elizabeth expected Lady Catherine to give her a letter from

Lady Catherine Asks Some Questions

Charlotte. But Lady Catherine spoke to her very coldly.

'Miss Bennet, I would like to talk with you – alone,' she said.

Elizabeth was very surprised, but she took Lady Catherine into the garden. When they had walked away from the house, Lady Catherine stopped, stared rudely at Elizabeth and began to speak. 'You must know why I have come, Miss Bennet.'

'No, madam,' Elizabeth said. 'I do not know why you are here.'

'Miss Bennet,' Lady Catherine replied angrily, 'I have something serious to say to you. I have always spoken the truth and I shall do so now.

'Two days ago, I was told that you, Miss Bennet, were going to marry my nephew, Mr Darcy. I knew that this could not possibly be true. But I decided to come here to see you. You must have heard this story.'

'No, I have not.'

'Then can you promise me that the story is untrue?'

'You are asking me a question that I do not want to answer,' Elizabeth said.

'I must have an answer!' Lady Catherine cried angrily. 'Tell me at once. Has my nephew made you a proposal of marriage?'

'You have said that he cannot have proposed to me.'

'Miss Bennet! Do you know who I am?' Lady Catherine asked angrily. 'No one speaks to me like this! I am Darcy's aunt and I must know what he has said to you!'

'I will not tell you. You will never know if you speak so rudely to me.'

'This marriage can never take place,' Lady Catherine said in a louder voice. 'Mr Darcy is engaged to my daughter, Anne de Bourgh. Now what have you to say?'

'Only this,' Elizabeth replied. 'If Mr Darcy is engaged to Miss de Bourgh, he cannot have proposed marriage to me.'

'His mother and I planned their marriage a long time ago.'

'You have made your plans,' Elizabeth said calmly. 'But I am sure Mr Darcy has made his own plans. If I am his choice, why can I not accept his proposal?'

Lady Catherine Asks Some Questions

'You cannot marry my nephew!' Lady Catherine cried. 'You have no position in society and no money. You cannot be part of our family!'

'My family is not as important as yours, I agree,' Elizabeth replied. 'But if Mr Darcy does not worry about this, why should you?'

'Tell me,' Lady Catherine said in a quieter voice, 'are you engaged to my nephew?'

Lady Catherine Asks Some Questions

'I am not,' Elizabeth said quietly.

Lady Catherine smiled.

'And will you promise me never to become engaged to him?'

'No, I will not promise you that.'

'Miss Bennet, I am shocked,' Lady Catherine said. 'But I will not leave until you say that you will never become engaged to my nephew.'

'And I will never promise you that. There is nothing more to say,' Elizabeth said, and she turned away.

'But I haven't finished yet!' Lady Catherine cried in an angry voice. 'I know all about your sister's elopement with Wickham. The son of Darcy's steward! The Darcy family must not be disgraced in this way'

'I will not listen to you any more,' Elizabeth said. 'I shall now return to the house.'

Elizabeth began to walk away and Lady Catherine followed.

'Marriage to you would bring disgrace on my nephew!' Lady Catherine cried.

'Lady Catherine, I have told you. I have nothing more to say to you.'

They had now reached Lady Catherine's carriage.

'I thought that I would make you understand, Miss Bennet,' Lady Catherine said. 'But, believe me, you will not marry my nephew.'

Elizabeth did not answer. She turned and walked quietly to the house. As she went inside, she heard the carriage driving away. Mrs Bennet was surprised to see Elizabeth come into the house alone.

'Did Lady Catherine come to tell you that Mr and Mrs Collins were well?' Mrs Bennet asked.

'Yes,' Elizabeth said.

Elizabeth had to tell her mother a lie. It was impossible to tell her the truth about the visit!

15
'My Dear, Dear Lizzy!'

The next morning, Elizabeth's father came out of his library and spoke to her. He had a letter in his hand.

'Lizzy,' Mr Bennet said, 'I was coming to look for you. Come into the library.

'I have just received this letter,' Mr Bennet said. 'It has surprised me very much. I did not know I had two daughters who were about to be married. I must congratulate you, Lizzy.'

Elizabeth blushed. Was the letter from Mr Darcy? If it was, why had he written to her father and not to her?

'You are blushing, Lizzy. This letter is from Mr Collins.'

'Mr Collins? What does he say?'

'As usual, he says a lot,' Mr Bennet replied. 'First of all, he congratulates me on Jane's engagement to Bingley. He learnt about the engagement from the Lucases. But Mr Collins then goes on to say that you, Lizzy, will soon be married too. I will read what Mr Collins says about the happy man.

'"This young gentleman has a fine house, a large income and a noble family.

'"But," Mr Collins goes on, "if my cousin Elizabeth agrees to this gentleman's proposal, she will harm our family. Lady Catherine will not allow this marriage."

'The man,' said Mr Bennet. 'is Mr Darcy! So now you know, Lizzy. It is Mr Darcy – the gentleman who despises every woman he meets. Aren't you amused?'

'Oh, yes. I am very amused,' Elizabeth said.

'Mr Collins has been more foolish than usual. How I enjoy his letters! And I suppose Lady Catherine called here to say you couldn't marry her nephew!'

Mr Bennet laughed but Elizabeth wanted to cry.

A few days later, when Mr Bingley came to Longbourn House, he brought Mr Darcy with him. Before Mrs Bennet had time to talk about Lady Catherine's visit, Mr Bingley asked if Mrs Bennet and her daughters would like to go for a walk.

Mrs Bennet and Mary did not want to go, but the others soon set out for their walk. Bingley and Jane walked so slowly, that they were left behind. Elizabeth, Darcy and Kitty walked on together towards Lucas Lodge. Kitty was going to call on Maria Lucas. Elizabeth and Darcy walked on alone.

'Mr Darcy,' Elizabeth said, 'I must thank you for your great kindness to my sister, Lydia.'

'I am very sorry that you heard anything about it,' Darcy said in surprise. 'I did not think that Mrs Gardiner would tell you.'

'Do not blame my aunt,' Elizabeth replied. 'Lydia was thoughtless as usual and she told me. I thank you for what you did for my family.'

'I did everything for you, not for your family,' Darcy replied.

Elizabeth did not know what to say.

'Miss Bennet,' Darcy went on, 'you told me that you disliked me last April. Please tell me if that is still true. My own feelings have not changed. But if you still dislike me, I shall not talk of love again.'

Very quietly, Elizabeth told Darcy that her feelings had changed. She told him that she loved him. She said that she would be happy if he proposed to her again.

Darcy's reply showed Elizabeth that he loved her very much. She listened to Darcy's words and was very happy.

They had a lot to say to each other. Lady Catherine had seen Darcy in London and told him about her conversation with Elizabeth.

'I knew that if you still disliked me,' Darcy said, smiling, 'you would have told my aunt!'

Elizabeth blushed and laughed. 'You know me well,' she said. 'You knew I would tell your aunt the truth.'

'My behaviour at Hunsford was disgraceful,' Darcy answered. 'I am ashamed when I think of it.'

'We both behaved badly,' Elizabeth said. 'Since then, I hope, we have both learnt better manners.'

'I hope my letter made you think a little better of me,' Darcy said, 'though some of it must have hurt you.'

'The end of the letter was kind,' Elizabeth answered quietly. 'We have both changed.'

'Yes,' Darcy replied. 'My parents taught me to be proud – proud of my position in society and of my family. And pride was my stron0gest feeling until I met you, my dearest Elizabeth. You showed me that pride could be a fault. You rejected my proposal of marriage and you hurt my pride. I had believed you wanted me to propose.'

'You must have hated me!' Elizabeth said.

'Hated you?' Darcy repeated. 'No. I was angry, but my anger was soon over.'

'How did you feel when you first saw me at Pemberley? Were you angry with me for being there?' Elizabeth asked.

'No. I wanted to show you how I had changed. I wanted you to think well of me.'

As they walked back to the house, they began to talk about Bingley and Jane. Darcy was very pleased about their engagement.

'I watched your sister carefully after we returned to Netherfield,' Darcy told her. 'I became sure that she loved Bingley. I told him so. I also told him that Jane was in London last winter. He was angry that I did not tell him then. But he has forgiven me now.'

That night, Elizabeth told Jane about her walk with Mr Darcy. At first, Jane did not believe her.

'Lizzy,' Jane said, 'you cannot be engaged to Mr Darcy. I know how much you dislike him.'

'Perhaps I have not always loved him as much as I do now. But that is in the past. I know now that Darcy loves me as much as I love him. And we are engaged.'

'Then I am very happy,' Jane said, 'and I know Bingley will be too.

'I have always had a good opinion of Darcy,' Jane went on.

My Dear, Dear Lizzy

'Now Lizzy, you must tell me everything!'

'Oh dear!' Mrs Bennet cried, as she looked out of the window the next morning. 'Here is that unpleasant Mr Darcy with our dear Bingley. Lizzy, you will have to walk with Darcy again, so that Jane and Bingley can talk alone.'

As soon as the gentlemen came in, Bingley smiled at Elizabeth. Elizabeth was sure that he knew everything.

'Mrs Bennet, where can we go for a walk today?' Bingley asked.

'I think that Mr Darcy, Lizzy and Kitty would like the walk to Oakham Mount,' Mrs Bennet replied. 'It is a pleasant walk and Mr Darcy will enjoy it.'

'But I would rather stay at home,' said Kitty.

'Lizzy, I am sorry that you will have to talk to that unpleasant man by yourself,' Mrs Bennet whispered. 'But if you walk with him, Jane and Bingley can be together.'

During their walk, Elizabeth and Darcy talked about the future. Darcy said that he would speak to Mr Bennet that evening and ask for his permission to marry Elizabeth. Elizabeth decided that she would tell her mother herself. She did not know what Mrs Bennet would say when she heard the news!

In the evening, Mr Darcy went to speak to Mr Bennet in his library. When he came back he smiled at Elizabeth and said, 'Go to your father. He wants to talk to you.'

'Lizzy!' Mr Bennet cried when he saw his daughter. 'Have you gone mad? Haven't you always hated this man Darcy? He is very rich, but will he make you happy? We all know he is a proud, unpleasant man.'

Then Mr Bennet stopped speaking. He saw that Elizabeth's eyes were full of tears.

'I love him!' Elizabeth cried. 'And he loves me. You do not know what he is really like. You do not know how much you hurt me by speaking of him in that way!'

'Lizzy, do not worry. I have agreed that Mr Darcy can marry you,' her father said.

Elizabeth then told her father how Darcy had helped Lydia and Wickham.

'So it was Darcy who arranged everything!' said Mr Bennet in surprise.

As Elizabeth left the library, her father spoke again, in his usual, teasing way.

'If any young men come to propose to Mary or Kitty, send them in. I am ready for them,' he said.

Elizabeth then went to find Mrs Bennet. In a very few words, she told her mother everything. Mrs Bennet sat very still and in silence. Then, she got up, walked about and sat down again. At last, she was able to speak.

'Lizzy! Mr Darcy? And is it really true? Oh, my sweetest Lizzy, how rich and great you will be! Such a delightful man – so handsome, so tall! Oh, Lizzy, I am sorry I disliked Mr Darcy so much before. My dear Lizzy! I cannot think! Three daughters married! You will have a house in London ... I cannot believe it! ... When I think of all that money ... I shall be awake all night. Mr Darcy must come to dinner tomorrow. You must tell me what his favourite food is ...'

'How did you first begin to love me?' Elizabeth asked Darcy a day or two later.

'I cannot say exactly,' Darcy replied, smiling. 'It was a long time ago.'

'You did not think I was beautiful at first,' Elizabeth said. 'And I was often rude. So did you admire me because I was clever and could talk well?'

'I admired you because you were intelligent, Elizabeth.'

'Oh, I understand you,' said Elizabeth. 'Women had always said pleasant things to you. You liked me because I was different. But you didn't know anything good about me.'

My Dear, Dear Lizzy

'You were very good when you looked after Jane at Netherfield.'

'Dearest Jane. Everyone is good to her. But you can tell me I am good as often as you want! And I shall tease you as much as I want!

'And I shall start teasing you now,' Elizabeth went on. 'Why did you not speak to me when you came back to Netherfield?'

'You would not look at me,' Darcy said.

'But I was embarrassed,' Elizabeth replied.

'And so was I,' Darcy answered.

'But would you have proposed, if I had not thanked you for

helping Lydia?'

'I had already decided to propose to you. Lady Catherine had told me about your meeting. She told me what you had said. I came to Netherfield again to see you. I had to know if you could ever love me.'

'Well, Lady Catherine helped us then,' said Elizabeth. 'Will you ever tell her?'

'I am not afraid of Lady Catherine, Elizabeth,' Darcy replied. 'I shall write a letter to her at once.'

———

Jane and Elizabeth were married on the same day – one of the happiest days of Mrs Bennet's life.

Mr Bennet was sad that Elizabeth had left Longbourn, but he visited her often at Pemberley. The Bingleys stayed at Netherfield for only a year. Bingley then bought an estate thirty miles from Pemberley. The two sisters were very happy.

Kitty often visited her two eldest sisters. Now that she was not with Lydia, she became more sensible. Mary stayed at home with her mother and studied. George Wickham was not invited to Pemberley, but Darcy and Elizabeth sometimes invited Lydia there.

Caroline Bingley had been angry when Darcy married Elizabeth. But Miss Bingley soon decided that she was still Jane and Elizabeth's friend. She enjoyed visiting Pemberley and spending time with Elizabeth and Georgiana Darcy.

Lady Catherine wrote a very rude letter to Darcy when he got married. For some time, Darcy refused to answer it. But Elizabeth said he should forgive Lady Catherine. And, much later, Lady Catherine was invited to visit Pemberley again.

Mr and Mrs Gardiner were always welcome at Pemberley. Darcy and Elizabeth loved them very much. They had taken their niece to Derbyshire and had brought Elizabeth and Darcy together at last!

Points for Understanding

1

1 Why does Mrs Bennet want her husband to call on Mr Bingley?
2 Who comes to the assembly rooms with Mr Bingley?
3 Why does Elizabeth Bennet decide that she will never like Mr Darcy?
4 Why does Darcy dislike most of the Bennet family? Why does Darcy like Elizabeth?
5 What are the names of the five Bennet sisters?
6 'One compliment does not always lead to marriage.'
   (a) Who is Darcy talking to?
   (b) Why does he say this?

2

1 Why does Elizabeth walk to Netherfield Hall?
2 Why is Caroline Bingley jealous of Elizabeth?
3 Elizabeth says, 'I like to study people's faults.'
   She says vanity and pride are faults. What is Mr Darcy's opinion?
4 Mr Darcy decides that Elizabeth must never know his feelings. Why?

3

1 Who is Mr Collins and what does he look like?
2 Why has Mr Collins come to Longbourn House?
3 What does Mr Wickham tell Elizabeth about himself and Mr Darcy?

4

1 What does Mr Denny say about Mr Wickham at the Netherfield Ball?
2 Sir William Lucas talks about a 'certain event' to Mr Darcy. Why is Darcy worried about what Sir William says?
3 Elizabeth likes George Wickham. What do Caroline Bingley and Mr Bingley say about him?
4 How do Mrs Bennet and Mary Bennet embarrass Elizabeth at the Ball?

5

1. Why does Mr Collins wish to get married?
2. Does Mr Bennet want Elizabeth to marry to Mr Collins?
3. Why is Jane upset by Caroline Bingley's letter?
4. Charlotte Lucas is not in love with Mr Collins. Why does she decide to marry him?

6

1. Why does Elizabeth say that Mr Bingley is thoughtless and weak?
2. Elizabeth's aunt, Mrs Gardiner, tells Elizabeth not to fall in love with Wickham. Why?
3. Jane goes to London with the Gardiners. What does she tell Elizabeth about Caroline Bingley in her second letter?
4. Who is Miss King?

7

1. What kind of person is Lady Catherine de Bourgh?
2. Elizabeth goes to Rosings and meets Mr Darcy again. How do you know that Darcy is still interested in Elizabeth?
3. 'My dear Elizabeth, Mr Darcy must be in love with you!' Charlotte says. Why does she say this?
4. 'Darcy told me that he saved a friend from a very foolish marriage.' Why is Elizabeth angry when Colonel Fitzwilliam tells her this?

8

1. Why is Elizabeth angry at Mr Darcy's proposal?
2. Elizabeth gives Darcy two reasons for disliking him very much. What are the reasons?
3. Darcy writes Elizabeth a letter. What does he say about:
   (a) Jane and Bingley?
   (b) Wickham and himself?
4. How does Elizabeth feel after she has read Darcy's letter?

9

1. Why do Elizabeth and Jane decide not to tell anybody about Wickham's bad character?
2. Elizabeth asks her father not to allow Lydia to go to Brighton. Why does she ask him this?
3. Where is Elizabeth going to go on holiday with her aunt and uncle?

10

1. What does Mrs Reynolds, the housekeeper at Pemberley, tell the Gardiners and Elizabeth about:
   (a) Mr Wickham's character?
   (b) Mr Darcy's character?
2. How do Darcy and Elizabeth behave when they meet each other at Pemberley for the first time?
3. Mr Darcy, Miss Darcy and Mr Bingley visit Elizabeth and the Gardiners. Why do Mr and Mrs Gardiner watch Elizabeth and Mr Darcy with interest?
4. Who does Bingley want to talk about?
5. When Elizabeth and the Gardiners visit Pemberley again why is Caroline Bingley angry with Elizabeth?

11

1. Elizabeth receives some bad news. What is this bad news?
2. How does Mr Darcy behave towards Elizabeth when he hears her bad news?
3. How does Elizabeth feel about Darcy now?

12

1. Wickham agrees to marry Lydia. What arrangements has Mr Gardiner made with Wickham?
2. Darcy was at Lydia's wedding. Elizabeth asks her aunt for more information. What does her aunt tell her?
3. Why does Mrs Gardiner believe that Darcy helped Wickham and Lydia?

13

1. Bingley and Darcy come to Longbourn. Why is Elizabeth upset by Darcy's behaviour?
2. 'Oh, Lizzie!' Jane says. 'I am the happiest girl in the world.' Why does she say this?

14

1. Why does Lady Catherine come to visit Elizabeth?
2. How does Elizabeth make Lady Catherine very angry?

15

1. That night, Elizabeth told Jane about her walk with Mr Darcy. What do you think Elizabeth tells Jane about her conversation with Mr Darcy?
2. How does Mrs Bennet feel about Elizabeth's engagement to Darcy?
3. 'Lady Catherine helped us then,' says Elizabeth to Darcy. What does Elizabeth mean by these words?
4. Which people visit Darcy and Elizabeth at Pemberley?

Glossary

1. **neighbourhood** (page 5)
   the area around the village of Longbourn.
2. **delighted** (page 5)
   very pleased.
3. **let** (page 5)
   if someone pays money to the owner of a house and lives in the house, we say that the house is let to that person.
4. **What a chance this is** (page 5)
   Mrs Bennet is excited. She is saying this is a good opportunity for Jane to get to know a young man and marry him.
5. **good-natured** (page 5)
   kind and friendly.
6. **fine** (page 5)
   you use fine to describe something that is very good. A fine house is a big, expensive beautiful house. You will find other examples in this book: *fine gentleman, fine eyes, fine food, fine furniture, fine manners* (See Glossary no. 21), *How fine it sounds!, fine character, fine young man*.
7. **call on** – to call on (page 5)
   visit. It was polite and correct behaviour for Mr Bennet, the head of the family, to call on someone he did not know.
8. **calmly** (page 5)
   quietly, not showing any worry.
9. **tease** – to tease (page 5)
   say something that you do not mean seriously. If you tease someone you laugh at them and try to make them angry. It is not kind to tease someone.
10. **severely** (page 6)
    very seriously.

11 **sensible** (page 6)
a sensible person is someone who thinks carefully about what they do and say. If you do something sensible, you do what people think is the right thing to do.

12 **gossip** – *... his wife's chatter and love of gossip* (page 6)
gossip is conversation about what people have done or have said. Gossip may not be true and it may not be polite.
Chatter is conversation about unimportant things all the time.

13 **humour** – *sense of humour* (page 6)
a person who has a sense of humour is able to see when something is funny.

14 **ball** – *assembly ball* (page 6)
a ball is a dance. An assembly ball was held in large meeting rooms (or assembly rooms) in a town.

15 **family** – *noble family* (page 6)
a noble family is often powerful and rich and might own a lot of land and property. A noble family has a high position in society. (See Glossary no. 38.)

16 **estate** (page 6)
a large area of land which is owned by one person or family. On an estate there is usually a big house for the family and also farms, small houses for the farmworkers, and fields.

17 **admired** – to admire (page 6)
like someone because of what they look like or what they do.

18 **proud** (page 6)
if you are proud you think you are better and more important than other people. (See Glossary no. 37 - pride.)

19 **amused** – *be amused* (page 7)
think something is funny.

20 **regiment** – *militia regiment* (page 7)
a group of men who are soldiers, but who do not work as soldiers all the time. At this time, England was at war with France, so the country needed soldiers to guard England (the militia) and soldiers to fight in France (the regular army).

21 **manners** – *fine manners* (page 7)
if you have fine manners you speak and behave very politely to other people.

22 **blushed** (page 7)
when you blush your face goes red because you are uncomfortable or embarrassed. (See Glossary no. 47.)

23 **opinion** (page 9)
your opinion is what you think about someone or something.

24 *plain* (page 9)
not good-looking, not pretty.
25 *expected* – *to expect* (page 10)
believe that something will happen.
26 *bowed* – *to bow* (page 10)
if you bow you bend your head and body towards someone when you meet them or want to be polite to them.
27 *engagement* (page 10)
an agreement that a man and a woman are going to get married. If you congratulate someone on their engagement, you tell them you are pleased they are going to get married.
28 *compliment* (page 10)
something you say to someone to show you admire them. You can *pay someone a compliment*.
29 *exercise* (page 13)
something you do which uses a lot of energy - like walking or playing a sport.
30 *settling down* – *to settle down* (page 14)
live in one particular place all the time instead of moving around. Mrs Bennet is telling Mr Bingley that he should get married.
31 *change my mind* - *to change your mind* (page 14)
decide to do something different.
32 *character* (page 14)
the way you behave, the things you like and dislike, the things you do and say and the things you believe make your character.
33 *looking forward to* – *to look forward to* (page 15)
think with pleasure about doing something in the future.
34 *dare* – *to dare* (page 16)
be brave enough to do something.
35 *punish* – *to punish* (page 17)
be unkind to someone because they have done or said something wrong.
36 *faults* (page 17)
the bad parts of someone's character. (See Glossary no. 32.)
37 *pride* – *vanity and pride* (page 17)
vanity means having a very good opinion of yourself. Vanity is always a fault. Pride can mean a feeling that you are better than other people. In this sense, pride is a fault. Pride can also mean a feeling of pleasure because of what you or your family owns or does. This kind of pride is not a fault.
38 *society* – *position in society* (page 17)
Darcy is saying that his family is more important than most other families in England because it is rich and powerful.

39 **inherit** – *to inherit* (page 20)
   get money or property from someone who has died. Mr Collins will inherit Longbourn House when Mr Bennet dies.
40 **clergyman** (page 20)
   a priest in the Christian church. A clergyman who is paid to look after the people in a certain place is said to have the *living* of that place.
41 **patron** (page 20)
   someone who pays all of another person's expenses. Lady Catherine de Bourgh (b3:(r)) is a rich woman who owns the estate, Rosings Park, at Hunsford. She pays for the clergyman who works at Hunsford. She can choose who gets the living there.
42 **income** (page 21)
   the amount of money someone earns or gets from owning estates and property.
43 **respect** – *to respect* (page 21)
   think well of someone.
44 **steward** (page 24)
   a person whose job is to look after an estate - the house, money, farms, land and all the people who work on the estate.
45 **event** – *certain event* (page 26)
   Sir William is talking about Jane and Bingley's wedding. No one has said that Jane and Bingley are going to get married so Sir William will not say the word 'marriage'.
46 **prejudiced** – *to be prejudiced* (page 27)
   dislike someone without a good reason.
47 **embarrassed** – *to be embarrassed* (page 28)
   feel uncomfortable or unhappy because you have done something wrong or foolish or someone else has.
48 **propose** – *to propose* (page 30)
   ask someone to marry you. An offer of marriage is called a *proposal*. If you say you will marry someone, you *accept their proposal*.
49 **anxiously** (page 36)
   if you are anxious about something you are worried about it.
50 **blame** – *to blame* (page 37)
   think or say that someone has done something wrong. If someone *takes the blame* for something, they agree that they did do something wrong.
51 **marriage** – *to make a sensible marriage* (page 39)
   Mrs Gardiner is saying that Elizabeth must marry a man who has money and property. She cannot marry a poor man just because she loves him.

52 **Lake District** (page 41)
a very beautiful part of England where there are many lakes and mountains. The Lake District is in the north-west of England.
53 **guardian** (page 46)
someone who takes care of a child or young person as if they are that person's parent.
54 **despise** – *to despise* (page 48)
dislike someone because you do not think well of them.
55 **accusations** (page 50)
if you make an accusation against somebody you say that you believe they have done something wrong.
56 **elope** – *to elope* (page 52)
go away secretly to get married. A man and a woman elope when they do not have permission from their parents or guardians to get married (See Glossary no. 53).
57 **revenge** – *to take revenge* (page 52)
harm someone who has harmed you.
58 **ashamed** – *to be ashamed* (page 54)
feel very bad because you know that you have done something wrong.
59 **heart** – *broken heart* (page 55)
if you have a broken heart, you are very, very sad.
60 **houses** – *beautiful houses* (page 58)
people who owned estates often allowed visitors to look around the fine large houses and gardens.
61 **housekeeper** (page 58)
a woman whose job is to look after a house. At Pemberley, the housekeeper was an important person who looked after the house and all the servants for Mr Darcy.
62 **shy** (page 63)
quiet because you are not comfortable when you are with other people.
63 **disgrace** – *Lydia's elopement was a great disgrace ...* (page 67)
Lydia's elopement was something which brought shame on her family. People no longer thought well of the Bennet family.
64 **deceitful** (page 68)
a deceitful person tries to make people believe things that are not true.
65 **settlement** (page 70)
an legal agreement about how much money Wickham will get when he marries Lydia.
66 **army** – *regular army* (page 70)
Wickham had been in the militia. See Glossary no. 20. Now he is going to join the regular army, so he will be a soldier all the time.

Macmillan Education Limited
4 Crinan Street
London N1 9XW

Companies and representatives throughout the world

ISBN 978–1–4050–7301–1

This retold version by Margaret Tarner for Macmillan Readers
First published 1993
Text © Margaret Tarner 1993, 2002, 2005
Design and illustration © Macmillan Education Limited 1993, 2002, 2005

This edition first published 2005

All rights reserved; no part of this publication may be reproduced,
stored in a retrieval system, transmitted in any form, or by any means,
electronic, mechanical, photocopying, recording, or otherwise, without
the prior written permission of the publishers.

Illustrated by Alexy Pendle
Designed by Sue Vaudin
Original cover template design by Jackie Hill
Cover illustration: engraving of Kitley House by R. Ackerman, 1828/Corbis

These materials may contain links for third party websites. We have no
control over, and are not responsible for, the contents of such third party
websites. Please use care when accessing them.

Although we have tried to trace and contact copyright holders before
publication, in some cases this has not been possible. If contacted we will be
pleased to rectify any errors or omissions at the earliest opportunity.

Printed and bound in Spain

2028 2027 2026 2025 2024
48 47 46 45 44 43 42